FATFACE &

FURBALLS' VERY

BAD FURDAY

Cass Clark

Enquiries: info@song-stories-and-stars.com
Web: https://www.song-stories-and-stars.com

Printed in the UK by Amazon KDP 2024
ISBN-979-8-5569468-9-7

CONTENTS

DISCLAIMER!

No animals or Time Travellers were harmed in the making of this story. Please think about it before you decide to have an animal or a Time Traveller. You become the only family they know, and they depend on you for their very life! (That's why Time Travellers rarely stay in one place for long – they are looking for a home). Any resemblance in this story to a real animal or Time Traveller – wild or domesticated – is purely coincidental.

To Mike – hopefully Gizmo would have approved this little tale.

And to Toby – sorry I had you neutered.

TO THE READER

This story can be read OUT LOUD∗ with your own interpretations of the characters' voices!

∗Perhaps not though at the following locations/times:

* Public Transport
* Funerals
* When your teacher is talking to the class
* A visit to the dentist
* When someone else is trying to concentrate on something important to them
* When you are asleep or when driving
* First thing in the morning when you wake up. ESPECIALLY if you wake up at 5a.m.

IF YOU WANNA DIFFERENT VIEW OF
LIFE, WALK A MILE IN SOMEONE
ELSE'S PAWS ...

PROPER CHAPTER 1 – THE ANIMAL SHELTER

"Oh, Laika! I do love you *soooooo much!*"

Fatface, the canine inmate of *Cage Number 6* at the Animal Shelter, stared longingly and lovingly up at the poster of pioneering space dog, Laika, which incidentally happened to be covering up the Escape Tunnel he'd been chiselling out for the past several months with his paws, under the erroneous belief that it would lead to freedom. (Actually, if he'd ever managed to finish it, it would have led out to The Shelter Laundry).

"Is it time for love again? You are so beautiful, Laika!" he swooned, as he gently stroked the poster with his big, clumsy, canine front paws.

"Love! Love! Love! Love!" he yapped, jumping around like an insane pup. "Is she smiling? Oh no! She's not smiling! No love, no love, no love, no love – arrrgghh!

Oh wait! Yes! Yes! She's smiling again! Love love love love …! Yippeeeee!"

In a darkened corner of the same cage lurked his reticent feline fellow inmate, Furballs, who had endured this display of affection on an often-hourly basis, (towards the poster, not him, he was glad to report), since their first capture two years previously when the Animal Catcher had hurriedly scrawled two random 'names' on scraps of paper and stuck them to the nameless strays' box, the one condition for entry to The Shelter being that you had to have a name.

In fact, they'd had it quite cushy these past two years since capture. Many humans had visited in the brief hope of a cuddly, attractive pooch or kitty to take home. However, one look at these two ragbags made most people either want to run, regurgitate their breakfast, (yep, there was still a bit of a smell despite the antiseptic baths), or simply walk away hoping nobody had noticed. To the outside world, they came as a package:

It's All or None. Two not One.

Yet, things weren't **so** bad here. Here's a brief update:

1. Weekly bath, (a hosing down with freezing water).

2. Food twice a day, even if you didn't eat all your breakfast, (which became your evening meal if you hadn't eaten it earlier).

3. Each having a soft fourth-hand blanket of his own.

4. Not having to clean up after yourself. (There's even a special toilet facility called The Tray, which gets emptied regularly whenever it's full).

5. And best of all – outside for an hour a day in a concrete area, known by all inmates as The Yard, for some not-so-fresh city air, which often blew a pungent wind across from the Refuse Centre next door. The whole exercise was referred to as The Daily, which included having to do your *'you know wots'* outside in the Tray, regardless of weather or temperature. Smaller litter trays were provided in each cage, but use of them was discouraged and limited to those little 'emergencies' that sometimes happen. (Enough said).

FATFACE & FURBALLS' VERY BAD FURDAY

Regardless of the weather, bedraggled animals would spend their daily hour outside either huddled together against howling wind, sleet and thunder, or baking on shadeless concrete during the long, hot summers. Either way, they were happy-(ish) to be alive.

The good people who work at The Shelter really love these animals, and do their best to make them happy, relying on the goodness of folk to keep things running. Most are volunteers, and it is only the Shelter Lady who seems to be the most frequent presence there. (In fact, she's there almost every day).

So, it's actually a pretty cool place, and better than *The Street*. Besides, most incoming 'guests' quickly find themselves a nice new home, with comfortable beds, rugs and log fires to sleep the cold Winter days away by. A *real* home, where you can come and go freely through fully-functioning, magical door-flaps that open on command, (due entirely in the animal's belief in its authority over inanimate objects, humans and anything that moves). Yet, the occupants of *'Cage Number 6'* remained:

CASS CLARK

UNHOMED.

Ok, so it wasn't much of a life. And, whilst beneath the fleas and general layers of dirt they seemed inseparable, in reality these two scruff-balls hated the sight of each other.

One thing and one thing alone was certain: *love* had never entered their experience, and today was no different.

"What did I *ever* do to deserve being imprisoned like a common criminal in here with *you?*" Furballs mused, glumly.

"Maybe you shouldn't have tortured and murdered all those little birdies and mice!" offered Fatface, from the other side of the cage.

"Hey! That's my *nature!*" retorted Furballs, indignantly. "I couldn't *help* myself! And if you're gonna play *that* game, then how's it that yooz are in here too, eh, you meat-eating dinosaur?"

"I didn't know my Mum for very long," said Fatface, as he stared into space, forlornly, "and never knew my Dad, or even an uncle or a distant third cousin fifth

5

removed. Don't you remember? When I first saw you with that dead mouse in your mouth, strutting along the street like you were the Lion King, I thought I was one of you! It was only after we were caught and brought here that I learned the truth — that you're a heartless feline! You don't need or care about anybody else! Whereas I'm a canine — a flea-bound mutt, and that means I need LOVE!"

"Oh, I'm gonna puke!" replied Furballs, hanging out his tongue and poking a paw at his mouth while pretending to heave.

"Suit yourself," said Fatface, protectively, as he went into his corner and flopped down onto his blanket. "But one day," he concluded, dreamily, "I'm gonna find a nice loving home where I'm treated with *respect* and have a proper name too!"

"I'm gonna have a nice loving home, respect and a real name," mimicked Furballs, mockingly under his breath, as he read his weekly copy of **'Scientific Feline'**, with its latest report on how the apparent superior

intelligence of cats has been used in training felines for space missions.

"At least I don't go all *nuts* around a slab of butter!" he said, coldly, without looking up but just loud enough for his cell buddy to hear.

Fatface ignored the harsh remark, albeit with a slight wobble of his bottom lip whilst he continued reading his self-help book, cheerily entitled, **'How to Like Yourself When No One Else Does!'**.

"Oh, to have my own catflap," muttered Furballs to himself, rolling his eyes morosely as he drifted off into a mid-morning catnap, where dreams of wild nights outdoors, terrified mice, fights over territory, rowdy miaowing, days in front of log fires with warm, cosy rugs to sleep on, food on demand, a proper name and yes, his very own catflap, filled his mind.

CHAPTER 2 – THE TIME TRAVELLER

It turned out to be a *very* short nap. The little communal TV set, hung high up on the wall just in front of *Cage Number 6*, was broadcasting some news story about a strange energetic force that had been detected by the orbiting INTERNATIONAL SEWERAGE TANK IN SPACE CONTAINER, or I-STINC for short.

The space station, first launched for purely scientific purposes and originally named the PLANETARY LABORATORY ORBITING PLATFORM, or PLOP, had had to be converted from a scientific laboratory to ... well, to put it bluntly ... you could say a giant *lavatory*.

The planet had been littered with so many poo bags, or 'pooperlooper bags' as Furballs liked to call them, which non-conscientious pet owners the world over had strewn carelessly about on their daily walks with their pooches that an *Off-World* storage unit had had to be implemented – and urgently.

For some strange reason, it had been decided long ago that 'pet poo' is best collected in a plastic bag and then thrown on the ground. The idea was that you then forgot all about it.

That was the thinking back then. Some protests had been made by fringe groups, most notably the 'RESPECT POO' activists who campaigned for many years to have pet poo restored to its proper place, that is: *buried in the ground as nature intended, (without a bag).*

'RESPONSIBLE POOP NOW!' and 'BAN PLASTIC POOP!' became international slogans around the world, as well as campaigning groups such as: 'POOP SANS FRONTIERS', 'FREEDOM FOR POO!' and even a political party named, 'The PEOPLE'S ORGANIC OFFERINGS PARTY of LONDON, ENGLAND', commonly known as, 'POOPLE'.

So, with such a build-up of pet poo-filled plastic bags, an urgent solution was needed, and the one place where we could all be safely free of the unwelcome side-effects of these non-biodegrading offensive eyesores, (*as well as all those nasty poo smells*), was ... well ...

OUTER SPACE.

As the two occupants of *Cage Number 6* continued their mid-morning snooze, the little TV screen suddenly flashed to an urgent message:

INTERNATIONAL SEWERAGE TANK IN SPACE CONTAINER (I-STINC) POOP BAY DOOR JAMMED SHUT. NON-RESPONSIVE. I-STINC AT MAXIMUM CAPACITY. DOOR RELEASE URGENTLY NEEDED SO THAT CURRENT CARGO CAN BE SAFELY EJECTED AND SENT TOWARD THE SUN FOR DISINTEGRATION. CARGO BAY NEEDS TO BE EMPTIED AND PREPPED FOR DOCKING OF NEXT SHIPMENT – PRONTO! BACKLOG OF POOPERLOOPER BAGS AWAITS ON LAUNCHPAD.

Back when the conversion of the space station had first been proposed, the human astronauts who happened to be occupying PLOP were not too keen on the idea of their astronautical living quarters being turned into a giant poo bag storage unit. But once it had been explained to them that they would be returned home safely well *before* OPERATION SPACE DUMP was implemented, and that subsequently the occasional emptying of the renamed I-STINC would be manned, or should I say *mammelled,* by highly trained stray cats – or Catstronauts as they became known – the human astronauts were somewhat relieved.

The News story went on to say that this storage method using I-STINC, (which orbits at an altitude of 400km), followed by the periodic release of its contents, had proved a great success so far, and that there was nothing to be alarmed about, which only served to make people on the ground wonder if they perhaps *ought* to be feeling alarmed about something.

All they needed now was to find the right catstronaut for the mission to fix the jammed Poop Bay Door.

And so, as the news story ended, the two occupants of *Cage Number 6* gradually roused themselves from their slumber.

"Why do hoomans leave pooperlooper bags everywhere?" said Furballs, with a yawn and a stretch, referring to the News item which had somehow filtered into his thoughts as he dozed. "My magazine article said they even do so in a forest! I mean, where's the intelligence in *that?*"

His query went unanswered, as a faint *hum*, at first thought to be some contraption or other that the Shelter Lady had often been seen manoeuvring around the place, began to fill the cage with an eerie vibration.

"W ... wh ... what's that noise?" said Fatface, sleepily.

As the *hum* grew louder, the two cellmates began to crane their necks around in slow synchrony to its source — the poster of Laika which, to Fatface's horror, had begun to glow a ghostly blue-white.

Their silent, quizzical stares grew into wide-eyed alarm, as every strand of fur stood on end, making the two strays look like survivors of a wind-tunnel experiment.

"I don't like it. W ... wer ... what's happening to her?" said Fatface, hoping Furballs would say something nice.

"I don't know," replied Furballs, with a gulp, wishing Fatface hadn't asked. "But it don't look good," he added, bluntly.

The floor was now vibrating considerably beneath them, making the litter tray in the far corner bounce around nervously, spitting out bits of dry litter-pellets onto the concrete.

As the *hum* began to whirr upward in pitch, the two animals unknowingly made little sideways movements in toward each other, their eyes frozen open and fixed upon the glowing light that pulsated with increasing intensity behind Laika, giving her an angelic halo.

"Are you moving in closer to me?" whispered Fatface, out of the side of his mouth whilst keeping his eyes fixed upon the glowing poster.

"No!" lied Furballs, indignantly. "Are you moving in toward *me?*"

"No!" fibbed Fatface back.

"Well, that's ok then!" concluded Furballs, as they both continued to edge closer together.

At that precise instant, the poster shattered into a million pieces as something burst through it, scattering shreds of paper over the entire cage in one giant plume.

"LAIKA!" screamed Fatface, as he lunged forward in a bid to rescue his heroine.

"NO Fatface! Don't be STOOPID!" squawked Furballs, as he grabbed Fatface's back legs with both front paws, claws extended at full stretch.

"But LAIKA!" cried Fatface, above the whirring din and almost blinding light whilst straining at his companion's needle-like grip and wriggling his rear end in Furballs' face, (much to Furballs' annoyance and disgust).

"OH! LAIKA! MY LAIKA!" he howled, frantically licking bits of poster from around his mouth whilst proceeding to try and put them back together with his big, clumsy paws.

"Nah!" said Furballs, as he casually released his grip upon Fatface's hindquarters, and sidled over to serve up his more usual dish of cold comfort.

"Doesn't look much like a cute pooch anymore, does she?" he observed, unsympathetically, as Fatface laid his *Contemporary Modern Artwork* upon the flat concrete. "Something's just a *little* bit off there," he concluded, with squeaky sarcasm, as he pointed a clawed paw down at one of Laika's eyes, which Fatface had stuck back next to her nose the wrong way up.

"Oh, Laika! I'm sorry!" gushed Fatface, feeling suddenly very alone and sorry, barely aware of Furballs' comments as he lovingly stroked what was left of his poster.

"Never mind," said Furballs, in an attempt to force himself to comfort his cellmate, "she was too good for yooz, anyhows," he added, finding himself unable to.

"Ahem!"

"Excuse me?"

Furballs turned to his lovelorn companion with a questioning stare.

"Wha' ...?" said Fatface, vaguely, as he hung his head forlornly, "... I didn't say anything."

"Yes, you did!" snapped Furballs back at him. "You said … *Ahem!*"

"I never!" protested Fatface, his gaze fixed downward at the clumps of gluey paper upon the floor.

"Well, if *you* didn't say it, then *who* did?" said Furballs, feeling more exasperated by the second.

"Well, *me* actually!" came a voice from behind the two strays as they sheepishly turned their heads around in sluggish unison. "It was *me* who said, 'Ahem!'"

The two captives blinked several times at what appeared to be a man standing before them. Starting at his feet, they studied this stranger's gangly torso in an upward arc until, with craned necks, their eyes met his.

"Hello!" he said, chirpily, down at them. "I'm a Time Traveller! And really I shouldn't have stopped here! But the fact is, I need the loo, and as yet the Universal Council of Longwinded Deliberations has not agreed on a Multi-Dimensional Toilet Facility for Time Travellers – i.e., no public loos in Spacetime!"

FATFACE & FURBALLS' VERY BAD FURDAY

Down at ground level, the two inmates stared blankly up at this intruder, their jaws dropping jointly as he made a somewhat unwieldy snorting sound.

"You see," he went on, "we now have a problem, in that in my urgent need to stop whilst superstringing around the Cosmos, I put on the brakes in my Time Machine and, well, I skidded a bit further into the future than I'd intended, and ..."

He paused momentarily, flung his large, red-velvet-lined black cape to one side, and sat himself down in the litter tray, which was situated beside him.

The two animals followed his movements mutually with their eyes, and again blinked in slight astonishment at the sight of an apparent *hooman* sitting in *their* litter tray.

"Does he not *know* what he's sitting in?" whispered Fatface to his companion, out of the side of his mouth.

"I'm more worried about what he might actually **do** while he's there!" replied Furballs, snarkily, through the side of *his* mouth.

"I only used it just now," gushed Fatface, humbly, immediately regretting his confession.

"Yeah, *thanks* Fatface for sharing," replied Furballs, a look of disgust twisting his features. "TMI," he added, faintly, under his breath.

"Goodness, this certainly is rather an *odd* chair, I must say!" exclaimed the Time Traveller, as he squidged himself scratchily around in the litter pellets. "It's like a sort of *beanbag* – without the bag!"

Again, came the snort.

"Anyway!" he proclaimed, bringing himself back on topic. "Yes! Where was I? Oh! That's it!"

He cleared his throat.

"Ahem!" he ahemmed, again. "Yes! I had gone a little bit too far into the future, and that means I've seen what's going to happen. And, well, of course I cannot *tell* you both what I saw there because that would really interfere with the course of Reality!"

The Time Traveller chuckled another snorty, hearty chuckle to himself. The two animals sat, frozen, blinking robotically.

"But the fact is," concluded the man, with a particularly stern stroking of his chin, "it's not looking especially good!"

He leaned forward, which made a sort of *scrunching* sound as he wiggled his bottom in the litter tray, causing the two animals to look on with a combination of trepidation, horror and disgust.

Removing his black top hat, the Time Traveller glanced quizzically – first at Fatface, then at Furballs – and queried:

"Now, which one of you two Sentient Beings is in charge of this planet?"

Fatface gingerly lifted his paw to point it at Furballs, who instantly hissed in disapproval, partly at Fatface's cowardly attempt to dump him in the deep end, and partly to make it very clear to this bizarrely dressed litter-tray-squelching stranger that he *wasn't* going to take any kind of nonsense.

"Sheeesh, what kinda weird *looney land* does this guy come from?!" he said, mostly to himself.

20

"Well, actually," came the earnest reply, "I don't really have a home planet anymore."

The two animals glanced at each other, sideways.

"Did you say that Fatface?" said Furballs, furtively.

"No, did *you*?" replied Fatface, defensively.

Slowly, they turned their gaze back to the stranger in their midst.

"*I* said it!" announced the Time Traveller, somewhat sensitively.

"So ..." began Furballs, pronouncing each syllable with the greatest care, "... yooz can un-der-stand, like, what I'm ac-tu-ally ... *say-in'?*"

His voice curved up squeakily an octave or two with the last word.

"Well, of *course* I can understand you!" rebuffed the man, with a certain frustration. "I have a Multi-Waveband Universal Language Translator – Standard Edition, of course. I'm not quite *qualified* enough yet for the Deluxe Edition!"

His voice trailed off, momentarily.

"Why?" he continued, somewhat warily. "Is there a problem with what I'm saying? Do I need to adjust the Frequency Responder Unit?"

"Oh, no!" insisted Furballs, involuntarily nodding in slow motion, as both he and Fatface began to edge and shuffle backwards along the floor, their fur bristling *Mohican* style over their spines.

"Well, indeed! You might *well* ask from whence I have come!" announced the man, raising his arms in a grand, expectant gesture, his cape fanning out like batwings.

A howling silence filled the cage, and, coughing a little to cover his embarrassment, the man swished his cape behind himself grandly and continued, undaunted.

"AHEM! I come from another dimension!" he proclaimed, impressively. "You see, each dimension is merely a cross-section of an even **greater** dimension! The three dimensions of Space and the fourth dimension of Time are just cross sections of greater realities – you know, in the way that a flat square surface could simply be one side of a cube! But if you

22

only lived on the flat side, you would not be aware of the rest of the cube! Do you see?"

No, they didn't.

Feeling more than a little frustrated, and even somewhat irritated at this lack of acknowledgement, (or indeed apparent intelligence from what he believed to be the dominant species on this planet), he forced an insincere smile and searched his multi-dimensional mind for a way to describe REALITY.

"Ahem!" he began again, as if making a big noise would ensure attentive listening. "You see, the way it works is like this ... there are ..."

"Are you one of those Time Lord blokes that I've seen on the telly?" came an intrusive interruption from a passing inmate on his way out for his 'daily' in The Yard.

The man went to continue with his monologue, but the question had jammed his thoughts, and for a small eternity he stood motionless with mouth agape. Shaking himself back to life, he squinted and scratched his chin, letting out a deep, ponderful, nodding sigh.

"Well ..." he began, reluctantly, "... er ... well ... um ... actually ... no," he said, finally.

"Worth the wait," said the inmate, a small cockney pug named Burt, in a voice far too deep and grating for his size, who proceeded to walk off shaking his head dismissively.

The man's shoulders sank visibly as he cleared his throat.

"I'm just a Time Traveller – Second Class," he said, forlornly, as he turned back to the two strays. "I'm not a Time *LORD* with all the mod-cons, movies, TV appearances and book-signings *THEY* get!"

The two captives swapped furtive glances.

"You see," he continued, "I shouldn't have really stopped here, and I've done this sort of thing before. Every time I stop somewhere, I can't help but interact with whomever or whatever I appear before. Unfortunately, this time it was you two," he said, somewhat unapologetically, and with yet another snort.

He went on.

"And of course, that in itself changes the destinies of those who see me, and potentially for the entire planet upon which they dwell. So, you see, I may have caused a lot of trouble for you both."

He leaned in closer, placing a hand over one side of his face, in case anyone outside should hear.

"The problem is," he continued, almost whispering, "the powers that be haven't yet installed any public conveniences in the physical universe. It's still in the *planning* stage of development, and as you live in one of the Time dimensions, although it's already happened in the non-spatial dimensions where all ideas start, it can sometimes take time – ha ha, no pun intended, (snort snort), before we actually see it in the visible. Does that make sense?"

"I guess?" replied Furballs, with an unconvinced, upward peep as he gave Fatface a sharp, forceful nudge.

"Mmm? Wha..?" spluttered Fatface with a jolt, rolling his eyes around as if he had not heard the question, (which he hadn't, as he was still lamenting his poster).

"You see," continued the man, standing up once again, "my Time Machine is not *actually* a machine at all – it's a small planet! I think you Earthlings call it *Pluto.* I hijacked it a century or so ago, as it really wasn't being utilised by any of the life-forms here in the way it was intended, and mistakenly I brought its orbit in just a little *too* close, and then of course you all spotted it back in 1930, by which time it was too late for me to take it back out closer to the Oort Cloud! So, I thought I would use it as a Time Machine, and hence I hollowed it out and converted it … you know … so it doesn't go to waste!

"Anyhow, it's rather annoying now that you Earthlings can see Pluto more easily with your modern telescopes and spacecraft. It makes it *sooooooo* much more difficult for me to time-travel in, and so consequently I have to go into the future to see what might happen *if* I were to time-travel in Pluto, and then adjust accordingly. But, as you can imagine, as I have to use Pluto as a Time Machine in the ***first*** place to go into the future ***just*** to see if I ***can*** go into the future, it all gets rather complicated! Ahem! Well, anyway, I'm waffling now ..."

Furballs and Fatface bobbed their heads in baffled agreement, like two nodding toys.

"Well, in that case," asserted the Time Traveller, as he stood up and brushed his coat tails, "I just need you to tell me where the loo is, and then I'll be on my way!"

Without saying a word, both animals synchronously lifted their front left paws and delicately pointed in the direction of the human toilets.

"Oh! And there's just one more thing," added the man, as he turned to give one final inspection of the hole in the wall where Laika had once graced her presence, and in so doing revealed an ashen-greyish patch of powdery litter-tray contents on the rear of his black trousers. "It's vitally important!" he declared, with emphasis as he shouted into the tunnel.

The two animals turned to one another swiftly, each giving the other a silent shrug, their expressions an open question mark.

"When I de-materialise and re-enter multi-dimensional SpaceTime," resumed the man upon turning back to his audience and pressing something on his wrist, "a Residual Hi-Flux Plasma Ball – an anomaly of Time-Travel Materialisation – will linger for a few minutes or so mid-air. It's perfectly normal with Time-Travel. But! *Whatever* you do, **DO NOT** touch it!"

"Why not?" shouted Furballs above a sudden, whirling din that sounded like a hundred jet engines and rockets all firing at once, and which had *wind-blasted* the two strays almost to the point of seeing the outline of their skeletons.

"Because ...!" shouted the Time Traveller above the noise, and with a slightly squeaky voice, "You will ..."

He stopped abruptly, and with a sudden, pinched look upon his face pressed his wrist a second time, and in a flurry of mutterings about finding the toilet in time, said:

"Ooo! Gotta go!"

And vanished.

"Er ... what the..." said Furballs, with a slight twitch.

28

Before he could finish his sentence, the whirling wind-blast instantly dropped to nothing, as did the two animals' fur coats, which fell back down flat upon their torsos.

"Hooman toilets are disgusting places!" said Fatface, as if what had just occurred was just a normal part of the day. "Hoomans oughta learn some *hygiene* like us!" he added, as he instinctively walked over to the litter tray and began to sniff where the Time Traveller had been sitting.

"Seriously?" sputtered an incredulous Furballs as he turned his head toward Fatface. "That weirdy, badly dressed guy who talks to us in purrfect Animal-Talk and who has basically told us we're going to **DIE** if we touch the Residible Hi-Flux Plazzy Ball-ee Thingy or whatever it's called, and all you can talk about is *toilet hygiene?*"

"Well, not *just* toilet hygiene," replied Fatface, mopingly, whilst scratching a solitary, despondent circle upon the floor with his front paw.

"What else then?" questioned Furballs, with a dismissive, impatient huff.

"My Laika," lamented Fatface, sadly.

Furballs was just about to launch a particularly hurtful – though in his mind, reassuring – sarcastic missile along the lines of, *"You'd never stand a chance with her anyhows!"* back at his cellmate, when something inside him just said, *'let it go'*, and instead he simply rolled his eyes, miaow-sighed, and prepared himself for a much-needed cat-grooming.

"Do you know what hoomans put on their fur?" he said, changing the subject, with hind leg poised high in the air, *yoga-style,* as he readied himself for his first of eight-times-a-day wash routines.

Without waiting for a reply, he answered himself: "They call it, sham-***POO***! I mean, why would anyone want to put *that* on their fur?"

"Hoomans don't have fur ... do they?" replied Fatface, scratching his head and feeling somewhat confused as he gathered up the remnants of his poster.

"Well, whatever they have on their weirdy bodies, maybe that's why they use poo then," deduced Furballs, scientifically. "They are so disgusting!" he added. "Animals, on the other hand, have dignity," he concluded as he flung his other hind leg up into the air.

"Yeah," replied Fatface, "like how you're now washing your own tush with your tongue! Now *that's* disgusting!"

"Maybe to you," defended Furballs, "but then you don't even *bother* with yours! At least I make the effort!"

"Effort? You *enjoy* it!" retorted Fatface. "That's why you spend hours doing it!" he added, feeling very pleased with his new-found insightfulness.

Furballs hesitated.

"Ahem! ... well ... it's ... *necessary*," he replied, with measured dignity, in a knowing feline whine. "But you wouldn't understand."

"And why's *that?*" replied Fatface, feeling cleverer by the minute. "Is it because you think you're smarter than me?"

"At last!" replied Furballs, with a burst of relief.

And at that, Fatface fell very quiet, as he sensed that something had gone a bit wrong between, *"... because you think you're smarter than me?"* and, *"At Last!"*

However, his ponderings were abruptly interrupted.

"AAAARRRGGGHHHHOOWWW!"

Furballs' head popped up from his cleaning inspection. "What was *that?*" he said, his ears standing to attention.

"I don't know," replied Fatface, seemingly unbothered by the distinctly female human scream, as he gave himself a good scratch behind an ear with his hind leg. "It seems to be coming from the hooman toilet that the Shelter Lady uses. Why would she scream in the toilet?" he added, as he focused himself upon the much more vital task of straightening out the ear that had turned inside-out.

A man's voice could be heard booming off the echoey toilet walls from within its locality, muttering apologies and politely asking for the 'GENTS' before vanishing (again).

"Ah, it's just that weirdy Time-Travelling Dudey Guy," said Furballs, nonchalantly. "Goodness knows *what* he was talking about when he was in *here!* But, well, he's gone now, so who cares! I guess he found the hooman litter tray after all," he added, with a shrug.

Feeling reassured, and forgetting all about the '**DO NOT TOUCH THE PLASMA BALL-EE THINGY**' warning, the two strays continued blissfully on with their own ablutions, as if nothing had happened.

CHAPTER 3 – THE PLASMA BALL– EE THINGY

Amidst the intense self-cleaning operation that had occupied both strays' attention, neither one had noticed the strange, glowing *orb* hovering mid-air just above and in front of the gaping tunnel-hole, which, until earlier this morning, Laika had been guarding.

It possessed a pulsating quality, and glowed with a warm amber and blue light, sending out little firefly-like sparkles around the cage.

One of these sparkles drifted down to where Furballs had settled into a post-wash catnap, and landed on his nose as gently as a snowflake.

"W ... what's this?" he said, sleepily lifting his eyelids and twitching his whiskers from side to side. A slightly alarmed voice came from across the cage.

"Why is it snowing in here?"

FATFACE & FURBALLS' VERY BAD FURDAY

The two animals sat up and stared, speechless and wide-eyed, up into the myriad sparkles that now filled the cage and were floating all around them.

"It's so pretty!" muttered Fatface, dreamily, as soft little snowballs of light landed gently upon his nose, making him sneeze as they snuffed themselves out.

"It's a dance of light!" murmured Furballs, unable to resist the feline urge to snatch at one of the sparkles with splayed claw, only to smash it into a hundred more sparkles, which in turn only made him want to smash each of these but finding he couldn't keep up as each sparkle settled on his fur and vanished.

Eventually, the sparkle-cloud dissipated, revealing behind its veil the pulsating orb of plasma that had produced the glittering display.

"Wah ... wer ... what's *that?*" mumbled Fatface, pointing his front paw robotically at the orb, just in case Furballs hadn't seen it.

"Oh, you mean *that?*" replied Furballs, as he extended his own paw at the hovering sphere. "I hadn't seen it," he muttered, acerbically, under his breath.

The plasma ball seemed to be levitating, suspended mid-air with a buoyancy that gave it a sort of hovering bounce. It expanded outward, and then retracted inward again as if it were breathing. There didn't appear to be anyone occupying it, but all the same it somehow gave the impression that it was waiting expectantly for something – or some*one*.

There were several spheres within the outer ball, and each sphere within a sphere shimmered with a transparency that enabled the two onlookers to see right through to what seemed to be an endless cascade of … well … more of these round thingies.

Despite his comments, Furballs found himself being drawn toward the glowing orb like it was the biggest bowl of gourmet cat food he'd ever seen.

"Remember what the Time-Travelling Dudey Guy said!" he warned, as he found himself unwittingly leaning forward and gazing deeper and deeper into the plasma ball.

"Whatever we do, we musn't touch it!" he added, in a strange and uncharacteristically monotone voice, his eyes fixed wide and open as he began to rock back and forth upon his haunches, matching the rhythmic pulses of the orb.

"No touching," replied Fatface, in a sort of parallel trance, and with an equally vague, dream-like tone whilst nodding in agreement and finding himself involuntarily drawing circles in the air with his nose.

In joint harmony, the two strays began to chant:

"MUST NOT TOUCH THE PLASMA BALL-EE THINGY!" over and over, as they both began to shuffle forward on their bottoms in a strange hypnotic dance, heading straight toward it, holding their front paws out parallel to the ground.

The glowing orb suddenly began to spin, flinging sparkly bits all over the cage and causing the animals' fur to stand on end, which only made the ball spin more wildly as if it *wanted* the strays to do the very thing the Time Traveller had warned them *not* to.

A strange vortex-like structure began to appear from within, like some celestial, sonic whirlpool flashing every colour of the rainbow in a continuous whirlwind of light and whooshing sound.

By now, both animals were so close that their fur shimmered iridescently in a pure, translucent stream of energetic particles that seemed to be appearing from other dimensions and being blown about by the sheer force of plasma energy coming off the ball-ee thingy that they weren't supposed to touch.

Distorted echoes of the Time Traveller's warning, (and Furballs' reply), reverberated around the cage as if Time itself were being regurgitated and played back to whomever cared to listen ...

"WHATEVER you do," it chimed, "**DO NOT** touch the Plasma Ball-ee Thingy!"

"Why not?"

"Because you will ...."

And on it went until the very tips of both animals' paws were less than a strand of fur's width away.

Then, in an instant, all four paws simultaneously touched the Plasma Ball, and it began to spin uncontrollably, firing out sparks and little blue-white lightning streaks around *Cage Number 6*.

"It's beautiful!" shouted Furballs, a look of sudden ecstasy stretching across his face, as his whole body jiggled about iridescently.

"I can hear music!" exclaimed Fatface, as *his* body in turn erupted in light-waves that made him look all bendy and weird.

"Yeah, me too!" yelled Furballs, as he became all the colours of the rainbow, and some new ones too.

"It's the music of the spheres!" declared Fatface, his eyes wide like huge saucers.

"It's like a big, crazy, beautiful ball of string!" echoed Furballs, hypnotically.

It is interesting to note that, amazingly, no one else at The Shelter appeared to have noticed anything unusual going on in *Cage Number 6*. The distant sound of the Shelter Lady talking to herself while she manoeuvred the noisy machine that sucked things up off the floor at The Shelter's entrance, echoed lonelily around the building.

The little TV monitor continued to regurgitate The News, unacknowledged, and next door in *Cage Number 5*, Burt, (you know, the little pug who asked the Time Traveller whether he was a 'Time Lord', and was unimpressed with the answer he got), was sitting with his cellmate quietly playing a card game.

"Did you just hear something from next door?" enquired his jail buddy, a rather refined blue-grey-with-black-and-white-spots Great Dane named Pertwee. In the background, a radio played a bland, instrumental version of 'How Much Is That Doggy in The Window', *Bossa Nova* style.

"Nah! I'm concentrating meself on the game," replied the pug, his eyes fixed upon his deck.

"Oh, that's odd," replied his Ascot-bred cellmate, concluding, "I suppose I must be hearing things! Oh well!" he added, before looking down and muttering at the bad card-hand he'd been dealt whilst the bland music continued, echoing distantly around the cage.

Back in *Cage Number 6*, though, it was anything but calm.

"We're being sucked into this thing!" shouted Furballs, suddenly aware that his front legs had been completely absorbed into the plasma ball-ee thingy.

"Oooohh ... wwoooahh .... nooooooo!" replied Fatface, seeing his own front legs vanish before his eyes.

He began to stutter.

"We .... shoulda ... listened ... to ..."

"... The badly dressed dudey guy," concluded Furballs, as both animals' coats bristled like shimmering rainbows.

"Is *it* getting closer to *us*? Or are *we* being ...?" said Fatface, as his whole body began to disappear into the plasma ball.

"Yes!" replied Furballs, agitatedly, as he too found himself unable to resist the orb's final pull.

"Huh?" queried Fatface.

"Both!" replied Furballs.

And as Fatface garbled a half-shouted, "What was that?", both gasped, as they submerged completely into the plasma ball-ee thingy, Furballs' last words fluttering around the now-vacant prison cell:

CASS CLARK

"Oh, my furry little ..."

CHAPTER 4 – SPACETIME JUST AIN'T WHAT IT USED TO BE

All went quiet inside the cage. Once again, the orb hung innocently mid-air, and any bits of Fatface's poster of Laika that still remained floated down to the cold, concrete floor in eerie silence.

Apart from the litter tray, which somehow had survived, *Cage Number 6* was now apparently empty.

"Are you in here?" said Fatface, a little uncertainly.

"Sure, *I'm* in here, wherever *here* is!" replied Furballs, sharply.

"Well, I can't *see* you!" exclaimed Fatface, insistently, a slight panic etching his voice.

"Well, I can't see *you!*" retorted Furballs. "So, nows you know," he added, with rising irritation, *"BOTH* of us can't see *NEITHER* of us!"

There followed a long silence, as Fatface tried to figure out what Furballs had just said.

"So," he concluded, eventually, much to Furballs' chagrin, "if both of us can't see neither of us, then ... does that mean that one of us can't see the other one but that the first one *can* see the other one? Or, that the other one *can't* see the first one, but the first one *can* see the second one ....?

And on he went ...

"... And if the second one *can* see the first one but only if the *first* one says something *before* the *second* one ..."

And on ...

"... And where *are* we anyhows? Why is it so squashy and bright in here? Why is it I seems to *know* what you're thinking, and what you're gonna say? And why ...."

And on ...

Meanwhile, a strange and unwelcome idea was forcing its way into Furballs' mind.

"Hey, Fatface," he said, interrupting Fatface in an uncharacteristically quiet, calm tone.

"Huh?"

"If you can't seez me, and I can't seez you, but we both know we're ... wherever we are ... and we're able to communicate with each other, and can, (unfortunately from my purrspective, I might add), hear each other's thoughts, and I'm saying all this without even opening my mouth – wherever *that's* gone – and it's all bright and squashy in here – as you say – then I can only conclude that we're *inside* the plasma ball-ee thingy, and it somehow **did** something to us. Capiche?"

"Er, yeah, I think so," said Fatface, feeling even more confused. "No, wait! What does 'capitchee' mean?"

"It's Kitalian for DO YOU UNDERSTAND?" replied Furballs, barely restraining his impatience.

"What's *Kitalian?*"

"Oh, must I explain *everything?* Kitalian is what they all speak in Kitaly! Capiche?"

"Er ... oh yeah! It's funny, but somehow, I kinda knew that before you said it! Even though I still don't really *get* it. Strange, huh?"

"Yeah — very, as usually yooz don't *capitchee* ANYTHING I says, me being an extremely well headucated feline. Anyhows ..."

"Ok ... er ... so ... what do we do?" said Fatface.

"What I'm suggesting," concluded Furballs, "is that I've somehow been *de-catomised,* as the Time-Travelling Dudey Guy might say, and you've somehow been *de-muttomised,* and ..."

Furballs' tone intensified.

"... Somehow, *both* of us has been *squashy-thingy-ised* and is occupying the same space in this weirdy plasma ball-ee thingy that ..."

There was a slight pause.

"... WE NEVER SHOULD HAVE TOUCHED!"

"Hey! No need to shout!" fired back Fatface.

Ignoring him, Furballs continued:

"And please don't ask me how I *know* all that scientifical stuff I just said. I dunno ... ever since we got sucked into this ... whatever it is ... I just *know* stuff I didn't know before. And I was klever even *then,* especially with my spellink!"

"I hear ya!" said Fatface, eagerly. "Wow, this plasma ball-ee thingy is making me feel the smarts truly! I actually *know* stuff now! Like ..."

He suddenly ventured off in an unexpected direction – what you might call a *stream of consciousness*.

"... Well, basically, what you're saying is ... the de-atomisation process that occurred when we both entered the Plasma Ball-ee Thingy stripped us of our physical anatomical matter and cellular structure and created a *Time-Matter Flux* which resulted in quantum discombobulation of the Spacetime Continuum?"

His voice squeaked up a notch at the last syllable. "Oh!" he added, "and not forgetting to adjust for the Retractable Time Displacement of the Cosmological Constant!"

"Er, yeah, it squidged us together," replied Furballs, flatly, despite being somewhat bemused at Fatface's sudden knowledge of Particular Physics.

"Oh," said Fatface, wondering how he knew all that stuff that he didn't really know. And if he knew where his head had gone, he would have scratched it. "So, that kind of explains why it feels so tight and squashy in here," he concluded, scientifically speaking.

An uncomfortable, silent tension began to build.

"It's like one plus one equals one," observed Furballs, deeply.

"I thought that made two?" said Fatface, though not being completely certain.

"Basically," concluded Furballs, in his most scientific tone, "yooz and meez is gonna be in each other's heads for maybe the rest of our now *extremely weirdy* lives!"

A long silence followed.

"So," concluded Fatface, at length and with great philosophical gravitas, "we're like one big head?"

"Yeah, that's right, my ole' jail buddy, we're *one big head!*" agreed Furballs, emphasising the last three words. "How about we get some shuteye, and talk about this more later?" he added, in his more usual despondent tone.

"Well, if I knew where my eyes had gone, I'd shut them," said Fatface, at a slight loss.

"Yooz don't got to take *everything* I say literal like!" said Furballs, using his bestest words. "And besides, I've never even *known* what I look like! I only know what *yooz* look like ..."

He paused momentarily, then bluntly tossed the word, "... *unfortunately*," casually into the mix.

"Well, the same goes for me!" spat Fatface, rather defensively, despite feeling suddenly sure of himself.

"No, wait!" he added. "I mean," he said, in his more familiar state of being *unsure* of himself, "the same goes for you! ...No! I mean ...me! ... I think ..."

"Yeah, I get it," said Furballs, dismissively. "Like I said before, neither of us knows what weez each looks like ..."

Fatface sensed Furballs hadn't quite finished.

"... *fortunately!*"

And so, eventually, off they went to sleep ... sort of.

*

(A few seconds later)

FATFACE & FURBALLS' VERY BAD FURDAY

(Furballs): "Can you PLEASE stop thinking about food!"

(Fatface): "I'm sorry, Furballs, I can't help it! I'm *hungry!*"

(Furballs): "I can't SLEEP with yooz thinking about sausages! And don't call me *Furballs!* It's not my proper name!"

(Fatface): "Mmm ... I LOVE sausages! And you don't *have* a proper name, like neither does me!" replied Fatface, in *his* best words.

(Furballs): "How do you get to be *hungry,* anyhows? You don't have a stomach anymore!"

Not expecting a reply, (he didn't get one), he pondered, longingly:

"Sheesh, this place sure makes that *cage* we were in seem like a wild savanna in Africa!"

"Yeah, it's like some crazy animal cage thing goin' on in here!" echoed Fatface, agreeingly. "So, what do we do now?"

"Well," mused Furballs, earnestly, "I guess the best thing to do is stay calm ..."

"Oh, yeah, that's a good idea!" replied Fatface, eagerly. "That's a really good idea …" he added, just to be sure. Except, he wasn't. "… How long for?"

"Oh great," said Furballs, groaning, "I get to spend eternity with *Einstein* here! I don't KNOW how long! Now please GO TO SLEEP!"

(Fatface): "Oh, I wonder if I'll ever see Laika again!"

(Furballs): "Did you not hear me?"

(Fatface): "Sorry, I can't help my mind – it keeps going all on its own."

(Furballs): "Oh, to have a catflap so I can escape from his brain!"

(Fatface): "See?! You're doing it too!"

(Furballs): "No, I'm not! I'm TRYING to sleep!"

(Fatface): "No, you're not! You're talking about putting my brain through a catflap!"

(Furballs): "I can't help what my feline instinctive mind is thinking!"

(Fatface): "Exactly! See? Your brain is doing it all on its own too!"

(Furballs): "Great! I get to hear *your* mind rattling on as well as my own!"

(Fatface): "Oooh, I wonder if we get fed here!"

(Furballs): "When will he ever go to sleep?"

(Fatface): "What time's dinnertime?"

(Furballs): "I wish he'd shut up!!"

(Fatface): "Hey! I heard that!"

(Furballs): "Oh, deary me, I'm so NOT sorry!"

(Fatface): "Just 'cos you're a smarty pants, there's no need to pick on me!"

(Furballs): "So, you admit that I'm the smart one then, eh?"

(Fatface): "No, you're just unpleasant!"

(Furballs): "Cool! And I save it *all* up just for you!"

(Fatface): "You know what?"

(Furballs): "WHAT?"

(Fatface): "I don't like you!"

(Furballs): "Ooooo, now you're really cooking! Don't hold back there, give it to me from BOTH barrels!"

(Fatface): "I'm getting out of here!"

(Furballs): "HOW? I mean, how's a flea-brained cowardly mutt like you gonna find his way out of *here*, wherever *here* is?"

(Fatface): "I … I … DON'T KNOW how … yet."

(Furballs): "Well done, Einstein! I mean, you've never done anything remotely brave in your entire life!"

(Fatface): "And you've never done anything nice!"

(Furballs): "Why, thank you!"

(Fatface): "That wasn't a compliment! HELP! HELP!"

(Furballs): "Oh, that's right, deafen me!"

(Fatface): "HELP! HELP! I wanna get out of here!"

(Furballs): "Who's gonna help *you?* The only one who can hear you is me!"

(Fatface): "HELP! HELP!"

(Furballs): "You know what? I'm getting out of here too!"

(Fatface): "HELP! HELP!"

(Furballs): "No! Don't help him, help ME! HELP!"

Amidst the din, a sudden ripping sound tore through the plasma ball, instantaneously ejecting the two occupants back out into their familiar cage, once again as two separate individuals.

"Woooaaahhh! What was *that?*" said Fatface.

"Er … I dunno," replied Furballs, not wanting to be helpful and finding himself more than a little unsettled.

The two animals turned to face the plasma ball-ee thingy and watched, dumbfounded, as it evaporated into nothing before them, making a slightly squeaky noise, like a balloon letting out air, and finally vaporising into nothing.

Several moments passed, during which a slightly strained mood permeated the cage, each animal reluctant to be the first to speak. Consequently, neither one bothered to, and shortly afterwards, (without even bothering to acknowledge the other), each went over to his bed, thankful to be himself once again, and slumped down for the night. (Just to be really clear here – AS FAR AWAY from the other as possible).

CHAPTER 5 – THAT'S MY COAT
YOU'RE WEARING

Furballs awoke the next morning, and through blurry eyes saw Fatface's outline over the other side of the cage, where he appeared to be standing in a rather unfamiliar posture, making a terrible retching sound.

Something about it just didn't look right, and Furballs quickly rubbed his eyes with his paws to wake himself up.

Wow! My paws sure do feel heavy this morning! he thought. *It must've been all that squashy-ball-ee thingy yesterday.*

Without looking down at them, he blinked a few more times to clear his vision, and once more tried to focus on Fatface, who had just regurgitated a gooey ball of matted fur and was sitting back upon his haunches, looking somewhat confused.

"Oh, you're awake," said Fatface, gloomily, seeing Furballs stir out of the corner of his eye.

"Yeah, and good morning to you too," replied Furballs, disinterestedly.

The mood was, well, somewhat tense.

"You don't look so good," he continued, adding, (just to be clear), "not that you ever really do."

"Thanks so much," said Fatface, flatly.

"I don't mean ..." began Furballs. "Well, yeah, I do ..." he corrected. "But what I really mean is ... arrgh! ... it's just that ... you really do look *weird* today!"

"Don't you ever stop?" replied Fatface, dimly. Reluctantly, he turned around to face Furballs.

"Crunching dog biscuits!!" he declared, startled, his eyes suddenly wide open, as was his mouth. "What happened to your feet? And your ears? And your nose? And your ... well ... ALL of you? You look like either a really badly drawn cat, or a fairly handsome mutt!"

"Well, sheesh, thanks for the vote of confidence," said Furballs. "I could say the same about *yooz* ..."

There would have been a dignified, reflective pause. Except that there wasn't.

"... And," he continued, as his voice gathered pace and rose in volume, "if it wasn't for the fact that you look so weird, then I wouldn't even be *bothering* to talk to you! You don't even *smell* like you anymore!"

Both animals, it can be safely said, were now wide awake.

"Yeah, well now *that's* settled," said Fatface, "I would have taken myself somewhere quiet for a good lie down on my own, except for the fact that I'm having a strange urge to go torture a few birds and mice."

"It's funny you should say that," replied Furballs, "as *I'm* having a rather – disgusting I might add – urge to sniff somebody's ... er ... bottom."

"Well, you can keep your *sniffer* away from me!" retorted Fatface.

"Trust me," replied Furballs, earnestly, "I'm quite disgusted at the thought, but somehow it seems *purrfectly* natural in some weirdy new way I can't fathom. And besides, it's no one in purrtiklar's rear end ..."

He suddenly looked a little sheepish.

"… just anyone's will do," he added, casually. "Plus! I really want to dig something up that I buried, but I can't remember *exactly* what it is or where I buried it …"

He went to scratch his head.

"Anyhows," he said, changing the subject, "what *were* you doing just now?"

"I'm not sure," confessed Fatface. "It was pretty gross though. This *thing* started coming up from my insides, and then out came this … this *ball* of goo and fluff. Yuck! It was disgusting … just like those things *you* usually bring up."

"Furballs," said Furballs.

"Yeah! That's it!" said Fatface. "This disgusting ball of *goo* and *fur*. And they named you after *that?*"

"Yeah, I guess," replied Furballs, with a disgruntled shrug. "And thanks again so much for reminding me what we felines have to put up with!" he added, with spikey disdain. "And like I sayz, Furballs is *not* my real name! Anyhows, why in the name of kitty litter did *you* have a furball? After all, you're an evolutionarily lower species!"

Having scratched his head, Furballs lowered his paws.

"Oh, ha ha," countered Fatface, "so to be more evolved, you've gotta puke up fur and gut-stuff?"

But before the argument could escalate further, Fatface noticed that Furballs had suddenly become very quiet and was staring down at his front paws with a look of sheer horror.

"These ain't mine!" he said, with a sudden low, shaky voice. "I recognise these paws! I know I've seen them somewherez before, and I've got a really bad feeling about this, but these are DEFINITELY NOT the ones I had yesterday!"

"What are you talking about?" replied Fatface, nonchalantly. "They seem pretty normal to me!" he swaggered, without even bothering to look across the cage.

"I'm not kidding!" juddered Furballs, as his teeth began to chatter nervously.

"In fact," suggested Fatface, feeling increasingly confident in himself, "they're just as normal as …"

He stopped cold.

"... mine."

Faces aghast, each animal gazed silently down at what he thought had once been his own front paws.

"Ooops," said Fatface, simply.

"Double ooops," observed Furballs, as a somewhat unwelcome lightbulb switched on in his mind.

"I know *exactly* where I've seen these paws," he mused, gloomily, as the fur on his face momentarily turned an ashen grey.

He lifted his head slowly, and with a grim accusation, concluded, "*And* I know *whose* they are!"

"Yeah, I'm thinking the same thing!" said Fatface, nervously. "Something in me says I just knows where I've seen these scrawny, skinny little sticks that you felines call *LEGS* before. *Eeewww!* They really are like weedy little twigs! And they *definitely* ain't mine!"

Furballs suddenly felt unable to get his words out properly.

"I th ... thurr ... think I've gur ... gorrr ... got your pur ... paws," he said, as he began to tremble.

62

"And ... I ..." replied Fatface, as he began to sway dizzily from side to side, "seem to haaaa ... have yooo ... yours ..."

A dizzying realisation began to dawn upon the two strays.

"I ... gu ... guess," ventured Furballs, not daring to look across at Fatface, "that ... m ... means then, that you've also ... gur ... got the ... rer ... rest of meez ... too?"

"I can't look!" squealed Fatface, slapping whoever's paws he had over whoever's eyes he was currently seeing through.

"Neither can me!" groaned Furballs, too alarmed to worry about his grammar.

The two remained in stunned silence for several moments, paws plastered flat over their faces.

The rest of the Animal Shelter continued serenely with its daily tasks, blissfully unaware of events in *Cage Number 6,* where a small, sonic eruption was about to occur.

"You ok, Furballs? ..." said Fatface, peeking through his paw-slits.

"I'm f ... fur ... ffff ... fine!" lied Furballs. "You?"

"I'm ... grrrr ... gray ... grrr ... ok!" lied Fatface in return, as he found himself unable to say the word 'great'.

Both were now trembling almost uncontrollably.

"Gur ... good then!" acknowledged Furballs. "We're ... bur ... both ... fff ... fine!"

Gingerly, both animals peeked through the gaps in their quivering paws, as a strange quiet descended momentarily upon *Cage Number 6.*

"Are yer ... yer ... yooz thinking what I th ... th ... think yer ... yooz is thinking?" said Furballs, through chattering teeth as he began to simultaneously blink furiously.

"Hmmmm ... mmm ... hmmm!" hummed Fatface, without opening his mouth, as he in turn attempted (unsuccessfully) to control a sudden urge to scream, which happened to be the exact moment Furballs likewise decided to accompany him in an equally long,

64

desperate wail that would have set the fur of every animal within hearing distance standing on end ...

"OOOWWW AAAAAAAA RRRRRRRG GGGHHHH HHH!!!!"

Like two deflated balloons, both animals then let out a frail, exhausted rasp, followed by an equally hoarse inward suction of air in preparation for the second blast of despair.

"**NO!!**" they groaned, as they flailed and writhed around. "**WHY, OH WHY?!!**" they panted, over and over.

Occasionally, one would look up at the other, hoping this was just all a bad *dream*, only to find that it was in fact a very bad *real* before resuming their wails and groans.

Eventually, however, all calmed down, due mainly to sheer exhaustion. Then, having caught their breath back, they each stared at one another, nodding in relieved agreement that this had done the trick and that it had all just been a bad dream … except that it hadn't.

"Aawww, man!" groaned Furballs, as he held his head in Fatface's paws. "I'm still over *there!*"

"And I'm ..." replied Fatface before having to stop and think about whichever bit of him was wherever it had gone to, "... I'm ... hmm ... er ..."

"Don't bother," said Furballs, with a defeated sigh. "Save those few thinking muscles yooz still got. It doesn't matter anymore, anyhows," he added, as he wandered listlessly over to his bed. "*Nothing* really matters anymore."

The mood in *Cage Number 6* was sombre, to say the least, as both animals flopped down onto their respective beds and stared dejectedly out through the cage bars. Familiar sounds of the Shelter Lady preparing tonight's dinner in the far-off kitchen, and Burt muttering during his afternoon nap, wafted back through.

"It wouldn't matter, even if that door was open and we'd be free to leave, we'd *still* be in prison!" moaned Furballs.

"And I'd *still* be without my Laika!" lamented Fatface.

"Nevermind that!" huffed Furballs, rashly. "We got ourselves a *much* bigger problem."

"What's that?" said Fatface, mournfully.

"Well," reflected Furballs, "apart from our current predi-cat-ment, caused by the plasma ball-ee thingy that we weren't supposed to touch that turned yooz into meez and meez into yooz ..."

He made a grand sweeping gesture at their respective bodies.

"... we're gonna need to find that Time-Travelling Dudey Guy, and get him to make another plasma ball-ee thingy so that we can get back in it and get all squashed up again and then be spewed back out — as yooz and meez is supposed to be!"

"I guess that's why we weren't supposed to touch it," offered Fatface, trying to be helpful.

"Oh, you think?" replied Furballs, barely holding back a particularly caustic bit of sarcatcism.

"Well, at least we know what we each look like now," shrugged Fatface, optimistically. "So, what are we gonna do?"

With his new, big paws that felt like thick mittens, Furballs rubbed his canine jaw, and, with a few philosophical nods to himself, drew in a vast swathe of air through his large canine nostrils. Then, with great emphasis upon each word, he uttered the following slice of deep wisdom:

"I don'ts. Yets. Knows ..."

CHAPTER 6 – THE PRESIDENT'S BROADCAST

A special broadcast, given by Earth's current president, was being aired on the little TV and watched intently by the occupants of *Cage Number 6*.

A new policy had been brought in several years ago, which stated that everyone on the entire planet would each have a turn at being President, swapping at weekends while everyone else queued up outside and waited their turn.

Of course, voting was always conducted in the fairest way possible, and everyone simply voted for everyone else.

Today's broadcast was being delivered by the brand-new lady president, who had just been inaugurated and was addressing the world's pooperlooper bag problem:

"... Ahem! The danger is that if bags of *pooilus stinkilus*, (that being the scientific term, I am told), are not deployed at a high enough altitude, they could quite easily fall back down to Earth by the pull of Earth's gravity and land on somebody's roof, or, worse still, on somebody's head.

"It is therefore imperative that the deployment is made at the correct altitude above our planet. Anything lower than this, and the consequences will be catastrophic ... Oh!"

The president stopped abruptly and held her hand apologetically over her mouth while her accompanying officials, standing nearby, merely shrugged their shoulders and gave each other furtive looks.

"Oh!" said the President, with a giggle. "I just made a joke!"

She then proceeded to elaborate.

"CAT-astrophic ... do you get it?"

(More giggles).

She turned to her attendees, who smiled nervously while trying to avoid actual eye contact.

"Oh, never mind!" she said, impatiently, and attempted to straighten her mouth downward into a more serious expression.

"I'm … oh!"

However, she suddenly blew a sort of involuntary raspberry through her lips, and became less and less able to control herself.

"Oh!" (Giggle, giggle, raspberry). "I'm so — pppzzffssszzz … sorry! Oh! Pzszpzszpzszpzszpz!!"

She coughed a few deliberate, hoarse coughs.

"Anyway!" she resumed, having regained a modicum of control. "This is a highly skilled and incredibly dangerous assignment, and the sacrifice that the chosen CAT-stronaut …"

She suddenly became quiet, closed her mouth tight shut, and lowered her head. However, no sooner had she done so than little snorting sounds could be heard.

"… As I said, (snort snort), it will … oh! … pzszpzszpzszpzszpzszpzszpzszp!! … It will be … (snort) … pzszpzszpzszpzszp! … (snort) … a very dangerous … pzszpzszpzszpzszp! … mission … (snort) pzszpzszpzszpzszp!! … and the sacrifice that the chosen … oh! I'm sorry! … pzszpzszpzszpzszp!! …"

Raspberries and giggles erupted into full-on belly laughs.

"... CAT-stronaut – ha ha ha ha ha! will (snort) make ... ha ha ha ha ha pzszpzszpzszpzszp!! ... will not be forgotten ... (snort)."

The President bit her mouth shut and sniffed a couple of long, deep sniffs in through her nostrils in an attempt to regain her dignity. One of the attending officials stepped forward and whispered something to her.

"Oh!" said the President. "I have to go now! It's time to swap Presidents!"

Preparing herself with a cough, she drew in a deep breath and began to make her official departing speech.

"I'd like to thank ..."

At which point the TV station abruptly switched straight to a new show about how rare exotic fruits are becoming extinct and how to grow them if you live in a city, the first episode of which was entitled, 'Last Mango in Paris'.

"What ... er ... was that she said about a *sacrifice?*"

Fatface, having consoled himself as best as he could by staring blankly at the TV set so that he didn't have to look at his own body while it was currently being worn by Furballs, reluctantly turned to face him, nonetheless.

Furballs, likewise not wishing to look at Fatface, forced himself to do the same.

"Ooohhhhhh," he groaned, "this is a nightmare!"

"Tell me!" lamented Fatface, shaking his head, knowingly. "But at least I get to see what I really look like!"

"So glad I was able to help you with that," sneered Furballs.

"I just never knew I was *soooooooooo* handsome!" continued Fatface, somewhat awestruck.

"Congratulations," said Furballs, blandly. "So, while you're busy admiring yourself, *I'm* gonna go do the hard thinking to try and get us out of this predicatment!"

Fatface suddenly looked a little subdued.

"Er … yeah … ok," he began, "so, then … what *DO* you think the lady meant by *sacrifice?*"

"I dunno," said Furballs, disinterestedly, as he strolled across to the gaping hole that now completely exposed Fatface's escape tunnel. "But I wouldn't worry, they're not gonna choose a scaredy cat like yooz!"

At hearing himself use the word 'cat', he groaned, shook his head, and placed it in his paws as he sat down at the hole's entrance, muttering to himself.

"Oh, man!"

"Hey, you just made a joke about yourself!" exclaimed Fatface, feeling himself to be suddenly a little bit clever.

"Ya think?" said Furballs, without lifting his head.

"And it would'a been kinda funny," continued Fatface, "if it hadn't been so MEAN!"

"Yeah, but who's wearing the *catsuit* smarty pants?" snarked Furballs. "And *my* catsuit, I might add!" he insisted, while pumping a big, canine paw a little *too* hard into his own chest and winding himself.

"Ow! Aarrghh!!" he groaned. "These paws are *way* too big and clumsy!"

"You be careful with those!" warned Fatface, defensively. "I want them back undamaged!"

"Well, *you* be careful with *my* catsuit!" snapped Furballs, getting more and more agitated. "So, like I said, *I'm* intending to sit here and think about how meez and yooz can get back to being ... well ... meez and yooz, so that I can then find myself a *real* home away from *you* and your stink!"

"Well, you do that!" said Fatface, woundedly. "And ... and ..."

He tried to think of something clever to say that would make him feel a bit better, but the words just didn't come.

"Yeah, that's right, you and your 'ands'," squawked Furballs, as he jumped up into the tunnel and began to inspect it. "And NOTHIN'! That's yooz alright – a big NOTHIN'!" he concluded, his voice echoing off the tunnel walls as he ventured deeper in. "You're a big fat lump of uselessness!"

"I know what I am! You don't have to keep telling me!" spluttered Fatface, protectively. "Laika was the only thing that kept me going ..."

He became suddenly quiet.

"... And you," he mumbled, almost whispering, and with a slight trembling of his bottom lip.

Furballs, however, had disappeared far into the tunnel, well out of earshot.

"All you ever do is try to be cleverer than me, but all I ever wanted was a friend!" Fatface declared to an empty cage.

His head sunk to his chest.

I'm just a big nothing, he thought to himself, sadly, as he picked up the few remaining pieces of the poster that had given him so much comfort, and tried (unsuccessfully) to stick them back together before flopping himself down onto his bed.

At least I had Laika – for a while, anyways, he thought, quietly to himself as he closed his eyes.

Soon, Furballs had returned from his tunnel inspection. Seeing Fatface asleep, (and snoring rather noisily), he slumped down upon his own bed with a yawn, and before long he too was sound asleep.

As evening drew in, the Shelter Lady quietly crept into *Cage Number 6* and gently removed the two uneaten bowls of dinner that sat dejectedly on the floor.

As she often did upon finding the two strays fast asleep, (which was quite often), she lightly tiptoed over, gave each one a gentle stroke down his back, and said, "Goodnight sweet dreamer, may you find a real home!"

Then, just as carefully, she left the cage, thankfully not having noticed the gaping tunnel-hole which had remained hidden in the darkness.

However, with a bowl in each hand, she found she was unable to padlock the cage. So, having had a long, tiring day, she took the bowls back to the kitchen, and forgetting to go back and lock *Cage Number 6,* instead switched off all the lights, left the building and went straight home.

Awakened by the sound of the Main Entrance being padlocked, Furballs wandered over to where Fatface lay fast asleep near the cage door, and noticed that it was still slightly open.

FATFACE & FURBALLS' VERY BAD FURDAY

A shaft of moonlight crept in through a high open window, lighting both animals with its pale, ghostly spotlight. Looking down at sleeping Fatface, Furballs now saw for the first time in his whole life what he truly looked like, albeit thanks to the plasma ball-ee thingy that he shouldn't have touched.

Yet, in the quietude, it occurred to him that if it weren't for Fatface, he probably would never have had any friends at all, even a not-so-bright one such as Fatface, or so Furballs thought. He didn't quite understand why, but a pang of regret suddenly tugged at him somewhere deep within himself.

"I'm sorry buddy for the things I said," he whispered, hesitantly. "To tell you the truth, you're the only friend I've ever had. I know you'll take good care of me, and I'll do my best to take care of you ..."

He paused a moment.

"... But I gotta go now."

Leaving Fatface sleeping, Furballs slipped through the cage door, bounded deftly up over the table and onto the window ledge. And with one brief look back, he scampered through the open window and out into the cold night air.

CHAPTER 7 – A GOODBYE NOTE AND A PAIR OF TIGHTS

The next morning, Fatface awoke to find a scrawled note by his bed.

He had always found reading a little tricky, so it took him a while to work out all the words, but he knew what Furballs' name looked like, and when he had got to the end of the message he peered over the top of the note and at the empty bed across the cage, feeling something was very wrong.

"GoN .... tWo ... fynde ... tim-travllin ... DoodEee guYie. Sinnd, Furballs," it said, in scruffy writing, with a big paw print at the end.

Fatface swept the cage with his eyes, periscope-like. Upon seeing the tunnel entrance, a pang of hope burst within, and he jumped up all excited and bouncy, and bounded over to the gaping hole.

"Furballs!" he exclaimed, in a scratchy whisper, headfirst into the echoing tunnel.

He did not wish to attract any attention from neighbouring cages, or the Shelter Lady, who in fact had overslept and had not yet arrived.

A dreadful, unpleasant feeling filled him on the inside, and as he stared into the tunnel's blackness, the thought of never seeing Furballs again filled him with a horrible emptiness. That, and the fact that he wanted to be back in his own comfortable canine body.

"Hey! Furballs!" came a familiar, grating voice through the wall.

It was Burt from *Cage Number 5.*

"He's not here!" shouted Fatface, back at the wall but stopping instantly, a sudden flood of horror welling up within.

Oh, creeping catnips! What do I say? he thought, desperately. *How do I speak like Furballs? Do I make that horrible noise they call 'MEEE-OWWW'?*

He went to speak, and all that came out was:

"MEEEOOWWOOOFF!!"

"Ok, suit yourself! I was just askin'!" replied the pug. "And where's Fatface, anyhows? And where's the

Shelter Lady? I need to go and do my *daily* and check my weemail!" he added, clenched teeth bared through gripped cage bars, *desperado* style.

Horrified, Fatface froze on the spot.

What did I just say? he said to himself, as he hid his head under a curled front leg.

Hope it wasn't something bad! he added, as he peered over his elbow.

Burt didn't seem too impressed! I don't know how long I can keep this up! Oh, what am I going to do? FURBALLS! HELP!!

Just then, the Shelter Lady began rattling her keys outside the main door.

Oh, NO! gasped Fatface, burying his head in his paws.

Frantic, he spun himself around and searched the cage for something – *anything* – that would stop the horrible swimmy dizziness he suddenly felt. Yet, the only thing that caught his attention was the slightly open cage door, and with that came something he had never fully experienced before:

FATFACE & FURBALLS' VERY BAD FURDAY

An *IDEA*.

And it was saying to him:

ESCAPE.

It was, to Fatface, about the scariest word he could imagine. His heart suddenly began to pound in his chest, and, at first, he thought something was wrong with it. Yet, something inside seemed to be telling him to jump through the open cage door.

Oh, Furballs! What do I do? he groaned, inwardly, as he heard the entrance door key turn and the handle go down. *Why did you run away?!*

His head suddenly became filled with all the things Furballs had said – things he didn't really want to hear right now:

"You're a great big nothin'!"

"You've never been brave!"

"You're stupid!"

"You're useless!"

"Why do I got to put up with yooz?"

And on and on …

It so happened that the only previous occasion where the cage door had been left open, and Furballs and Fatface had 'escaped', (well, they had run up and down the corridor while being chased by the Shelter Lady, causing a riot with all the other inmates barking and miaowing and banging their food bowls on their cage bars), had involved a rather unpleasant experience with some strange things that some humans wear upon their legs, bizarrely named:

TIGHTS.

It had been the only means available, (although no one knows quite why), and had involved both animals being 'captured' with each one's head caught in one of the legs of said pair of tights, making them look like common criminals, and which created some uncontrolled hilarity among fellow inmates, especially when the two escapees had both tried to run in opposite directions. The final humiliation had come with both being dragged back to their cage in front of all the other inmates – no doubt as an example and warning to all.

FATFACE & FURBALLS' VERY BAD FURDAY

Needless to say, Fatface and Furballs had become the joke of The Shelter, and as per usual they had blamed each other, (although Furballs blamed Fatface a lot more).

Ever since that day, 'THE TIGHTS' had been used as a subtle threat whenever any animal's behaviour was deemed unacceptable, and the Shelter Lady could often be seen casually parading up and down outside the cages, nonchalantly dangling a pair of tights over her shoulder, nodding to herself and raising a knowing eyebrow.

"Oh no! Not THE TIGHTS!" had become a Shelter catchphrase, as invariably that is what was said upon capture after an attempted escape. And it induced fear the likes of which no free animal in the outside world could have ever imagined.

Unsurprisingly, this thought was currently uppermost in Fatface's mind as he stared at the open door.

He knew how mean Furballs could be, but he also knew that Furballs had been his one and only friend, and it dawned upon him that he was now – at least only temporarily he hoped – a fully-fledged *felis catus domesticus,* (that being the technical, scientifical name for a domestical pusscat). And, although it generally would never have been of any interest to Fatface, he had unfortunately now realised that he *was* one! And that meant at least one good thing …

I can jump, and I can land on my feet from a great height.

Well, ok, so that's *two* things, and he wasn't particularly keen on the second half.

The main entrance door began to creak open, and an uncomfortable wriggly feeling churned in Fatface's tummy. For he knew that as soon as the Shelter Lady saw the open cage, she would lock it up – with him inside.

Hearing her footsteps as she shuffled about, fumbling with her keys, he said to himself:

It's now or never!

Without taking his eyes off the cage door, he walked calmly over to it and stopped just before it. Tormenting thoughts raged through his mind:

What if she sees you in the corridor?

What if Burt next door sees you, starts barking and raises the alarm?

What are you going to do once you're in the corridor?

Who do yooz think yooz are anyways?

What if you never find Furballs and the Time-Travelling Dudey Guy, and you have to stay as a cat the rest of your life?

If you get caught, you'll be punished!

*Remember: **THE TIGHTS!***

"I can do this!" he said, determinedly.

And despite all the noise going on in his head, Fatface found himself walking calmly through the open cage door, straight out into the corridor.

Wow! I did it! he said to himself, with momentary jubilation. *I feel like I've just walked through a wall!*

He stuck his tail proudly up in the air, and glanced down the dimly lit passage to the main entrance just as it opened and flooded the corridor with bright daylight.

The Shelter Lady appeared within this light, eclipsing it like a giant monolith as she stepped inside. Something within Fatface told him he had to act, and quickly.

Don't look back into the dark cage! he thought to himself.

He glanced around and saw the table, the window ledge, and the high-up open window. And he felt an urge to jump.

Ok, here goes!

Just then came a voice.

"Hey Furballs! Where are yooz going? Fatface just said you weren't here!" yapped Burt, as he poked his nose through *Cage Number 5's* bars, holding on with his front paws and standing on his back legs at full stretch, (which, in all honesty, hadn't made much difference to his height).

"Er …" replied Fatface, with his back to Burt as he hunched himself in ready-to-jump position, "… I … er …"

I don't have time for this! he thought to himself.

And before he could start to fret, another idea welled up within.

"Oh look! There's the Shelter Lady! …" he shouted, in his best Furballs voice, sticking out a back leg to indicate the opposite end of the corridor. "… And that means breakfast!"

At the word 'breakfast' Burt instantly swung his head around, and seeing the Shelter Lady head toward the kitchen, he began to bark.

Fatface, meanwhile, had noticed that the Shelter Lady wasn't alone. There appeared to be a man with her who was carrying something that had a familiar – yet sinister – shape to it, and which gave Fatface a distinctly unpleasant feeling.

Squinting to get a better look, he very quicky realised he was also being scrutinized. The man carrying the unpleasant *something* had spotted him and was walking slowly toward him, bending over and holding out his hand whilst rubbing his thumb and forefingers together and making a strange, squeaky, sucking sound with his mouth.

"Here, puss puss!" he said, followed by the weird squeak.

"I ain't no puss!" miaowed Fatface, defiantly.

"Here, kitty kitty!" beckoned the man, as he got closer and closer. "Awww, is the little kitty afraid of the friendly man?" he said.

Fatface remained unconvinced about the 'friendly' part.

"I'm warning you!" he miaowed, displaying his fang-like feline teeth with a hiss.

"Oh, my! You *do* make a lot of noise!" said the man, in a soft yet thinly-disguised ominous tone, as he proceeded to close the gap between them.

"No, really!" urged Fatface, as he began to panic. "You don't understand! I'm really a dog!" he miaowed, as he began to edge his way backwards. "I'm serious!" he added, with a particularly wild miaow. "This ... this

..." he stuttered, agitatedly, "... *CAT BAG* I'm wearing, really doesn't belong to me!"

The man closed in further.

Why ain't he listening? thought Fatface. *Ain't I talking plain like?*

"Ok, dogs bark, right?" he said, in an attempt to reason with this apparently *unreasonable* hooman, whilst the man continued to edge him into a corner.

Not waiting for an answer, Fatface drew in a deep breath, and thought as many 'dog' thoughts as he could muster.

Come on Fatface! It's 'woof woof', he said to himself, over and over. *How comes it's so **easy** to do it in my head? Ok, here goes ...*

"MMMIIIIIAAAAAOOOOWWW!!" he squawked, outwardly, with a grating rasp.

Oh man! he groaned, inwardly.

At that moment, he remembered what the *something* that the man was carrying meant:

PRISON.

He made a frantic surveillance sweep. Yet, the only thing that came into view was *Cage Number 6* and its open door.

I'm not going back in there! he said to himself, defiantly, as he began to frantically tug and pull at his fur coat.

"Look! ..." he pleaded, "... this ain't mine! The real me is underneath this!"

The thing the man was carrying was the same shaped thing that he and Furballs had been captured in all those full moons ago. It had been a bad enough experience *then,* but to go through it all again *now,* with everyone else thinking you're 'Furballs the cat' when you're actually 'Fatface the pooch', was too unbearable to even contemplate.

He noticed some writing on the side of the box, and despite his spelling not being too wonderful, (although he'd always done his best), he managed to make out the letters: **N A S S A**

It stood for the '**National Animal Secret Space Agency**', and Fatface knew this meant only one thing:

Catstronaut Training School!

A strange churning sensation curdled in his tummy, and he suddenly felt rather weak and dizzy, as, having seen the latest News on TV, he was more than aware that NASSA was looking to recruit some catstronaut candidates and choose one for the mission to fix the jammed I-STINC Poop Bay Door.

Backed into a corner, he made the most vicious wild catface he could muster, splaying his claws while baring his teeth and hissing at the man, who simply stood like a calm statue, tilting his head quizzically until Fatface finally exhausted himself and slumped defeatedly at the man's feet, gazing helplessly back up at the towering giant before him.

The man, in return, merely smiled and sighed.

"Don't worry," he said, with a gentle yet unapologetic laugh, "with that temper it's unlikely they'll select you!"

Good! thought Fatface, belligerently.

"But," continued the man, "they're fairly low on candidates, and one thing you certainly have in your favour is that you got guts! You're a brave little fellow!"

Despite feeling thoroughly deflated, those last words had caught Fatface's attention, and he looked up at the man, somewhat surprised.

"Me? Brave?" he miaowed, with big, wide saucer eyes.

The man smiled down at him.

"If they *do* pick you, I'm sure they'll do their best to bring you back in one piece."

Yeah, but that's just the problem, thought Fatface, dryly. *I'm in the **wrong** piece ...*

"Hey, I'm just the delivery boy here!" continued the man, with a sudden burst. "I don't know what goes on at the Training Centre! But I *do* know you're a very brave little fellow, and you might even end up an international hero!"

Somehow, this didn't comfort Fatface.

Reluctantly, he allowed the man to gently haul him up off the floor by the scruff of his neck and lower him into the box. With a grimace, he heard the familiar clunk of a padlock, followed by the dizzying sensation of being swung up into the air.

FATFACE & FURBALLS' VERY BAD FURDAY

As the man carried him back down through the corridor, Fatface poked as much of his head as he could through the little cage bars, and stared gauntly out, taking one last look at the surroundings that had been his home for the past two or so years.

"Bye Furballs," said Burt, flatly, as Fatface swung inelegantly past *Cage Number 5*.

"Bye Burt. Bye Pertwee," groaned Fatface, with a defeated, resigned sigh.

CHAPTER 8 – THE LORRY & A VERY IMPORTANT TV NEWS ANNOUNCEMENT

There had been no time to stop, despite the fact that Furballs was enjoying trotting along, alone but free.

The night air smelled fresh and new under the moonlight, and as he bounded away from The Shelter, along the path past the Refuse Centre and on towards the city, he thought about the events of the previous day or so as his mind whirred with questions and ideas in his new-found freedom.

However, one particular thought would not leave him alone, and tugged at his insides with a deep pang, causing him to stop for one last look back before The Shelter was completely out of sight.

I hope Fatface doesn't get rehomed ... well not until I can find this Time-Travelling Dudey Guy and bring him back to The Shelter before they know I've gone, he thought, as he turned away and resumed his jog.

FATFACE & FURBALLS' VERY BAD FURDAY

I'm hoping Fatface can cover for me. For that matter, I hope he can read my note ...

It wasn't simply that he wanted his own body back, but some unnameable sense of regret had swept through him.

I only got one friend in this whole Universe, and although I hate to admit it, it's Fatface.

Yet, he'd made the choice to leave, for he knew he was on an important mission and that there wasn't much time. So, leaving The Shelter, Burt, Pertwee, Fatface, and (thankfully) *The Tights* behind, he pressed onwards.

The approaching city had begun to awaken, and Furballs soon found himself increasingly surrounded by the hustle and bustle of noise and activity. Traffic rattled by, and occasionally a large truck or lorry would blast its way past him, brushing his fur back the wrong way and almost blowing him over.

He soon found though that miaowing back at these monstrosities had little – if any – effect upon them as they rumbled on to who knows where. Worse still, he found his *miaows* had unwittingly turned into coarse, rather grating *barks*.

However, unsatisfied at this blatantly disrespectful traffic behaviour, Furballs determined to show the next large truck who was boss, and at the distant sight of an oncoming lorry, he calmly walked out into the road and sat right in its path.

I've never backed down from a fight, and I ain't gonna start now! I don't care how big and square and weird looking this strange animaloid is! I'll show him! he asserted, with gritty resolve.

The oncoming truck began to make a loud noise and showed no sign of slowing.

Huh! He's just bluffing! thought Furballs, defiantly.

He puffed out his chest and stared directly at the two bright eyes on the front of the truck's face which, oddly, began to open and close.

Furballs inclined his head, quizzically.

Why's he blinking at me? he thought, as the lorry driver, having seen Furballs sitting in the road, had begun to flash his headlights on and off as a warning that perhaps he *wasn't* going to stop after all, and that Furballs might want to consider … well … *moving*.

"You'll have to move first!" he growled, as the truck steamed directly at him, blasting its horn and flashing its lights frantically. *I'll show him!* he threatened, inwardly.

Making a quick revision of his tactical calculations, Furballs splayed his paws out in a show of supreme power, anchoring himself down upon the tarmac in full *attack* mode.

I ain't movin'! he warned, finally, giving the monster one last chance to back down.

Missing his ears by a whisker and thrusting his fur backwards with such a gust that Furballs momentarily wondered if he might lose his coat altogether and end up naked, the lorry, with its big tyres and high-up driver's cab, careened right over his head, horn blaring, and then roared away without even stopping to acknowledge its obvious defeat.

As the marauding beast fled, Furballs spun himself around.

"Coward! Yeah, ya big jelly! Go on! Run away! Couldn't even manage to steal my coat!" he barked. "You're purrrrr...thetic! That's right! PURR. THET. ICK! Yer big fleabag! Run away and don't come back!"

What a big wimp! he thought, shaking his head in disgust as he brushed himself off and hopped back onto the pathway, albeit keeping a little farther back from the kerb.

Feeling victory was his, Furballs scampered along and began to ponder upon how those bona fide pooches – lucky enough to be rescued from The Shelter – are usually accompanied by their new owners, and that he – by his act of 'jail-breaking' – may attract attention of the *wrong* kind and find himself *re-rescued* by some well-meaning human, who would no doubt take him back to The Shelter believing they were doing the 'right thing'.

With that in mind, he continued cautiously along the path, dodging in and out of hedgerows and bushes, occasionally ducking behind a bin or a tree until, eventually, he came across something that caught his attention and which forced him back out into the open.

His plan upon leaving The Shelter had been to go to the city to see if the Time Traveller had left his contact details anywhere.

Furballs knew that humans not only talk to each other, but that they often talk to inanimate objects too, some of which – like the small Shelter TV set or *Talking Picture Box* as Furballs called it – also talk back to humans. So, being the smart feline that he is, he deduced that *maybe* there might be more of these Talking Picture Boxes in the city, and that one of them might be able to tell him how to reach the Time Traveller with his very urgent message.

With this in mind, he prepared some questions, and eventually found himself standing outside a shop window, the other side of which housed literally *hundreds* of Talking Picture Boxes, all having lively conversations with each other, or so it seemed to Furballs.

He sat down by the shop window and thought he'd be less noticeable if he acted as if he were waiting for his 'hooman'. Whilst people walked in and out of the shop, one or two passers-by made cooing noises and petted him, calling him a 'cute puppy', much to his disgust, (although he *did* like the petting bit).

*Remember you're Furballs the **CAT!*** he said to himself, emphatically, as he stared at his canine reflection.

Focus Furballs! We got a mission to accomplish here! Now, which one of these Picture Boxes do I talk to?

He gazed from TV screen to TV screen, each one chattering away to itself.

*Sheesh! Do they **ever** stop?*

He'd remembered that the one at The Shelter didn't talk *all* the time, and sometimes it was asleep. And so, he waited until things had quietened down a bit, and took his chance to speak.

Ok, I think I'll try that one in the middle first, he decided.

"Hey! Can you tell me where do Time-Travelling Dudey Guys go when they're not ... well ... time travelling?" he barked, through the window and at the biggest TV screen.

Some humans passed by, and commented:

"Oh look, the cute doggy is talking to the TV!"

This was followed by the kind of noise that Furballs had often heard humans make – usually at his expense.

Go ahead and laugh, lady! he said to himself, scathingly.

Ok, back to business.

"Do you know where I will find the Time-Travelling Dudey Guy?" he barked again, this time to a medium-sized TV screen, which continued babbling about something that had little to do with time-travel, much to Furballs' distaste.

"Yeah, thanks for nothing!" he barked, shaking his head.

Ok, I'll try another one. How about that one over there?

"Hey! Have you seen any Time-Travelling Dudey Guys? And if so, do you know where I can find one?"

Once again, there came no reply – just a continual stream of nonsensical noise.

Arrghh! This is worse than trying to talk to Fatface!

His attention was abruptly drawn to a small crowd, which had appeared in the window's reflection behind him and which had begun to make chuckling noises in his direction.

This ain't good, he said to himself, pensively, as he kept his face toward the window.

Just keep really still, and maybe they'll go away! he hoped.

What's so funny about meez talking to one of those Talking Picture Box things anyhows? Hoomans do it all the time ...

He decided to lie down and hide his head beneath his floppy ears, just in case someone from The Shelter might pass by and recognise ... well, Fatface.

And if any of these bozos try anything funny, he threatened, inwardly, *I'll claw their furless hides with my sharp feline ... oh, wait, no ... with my big, fat, clumsy canine ... paws ...*

He groaned.

Well, maybe not.

The News item on the large TV screen had flashed to an urgent report on the scheduled spaceflight to the I-STINC space station and the rigorous selection process of the potential candidates. Almost every TV screen in the shop had now switched to the News story, and the small crowd, which had inexplicably ballooned in size, clustered itself around the shop window, trapping Furballs who, turning hesitantly, gingerly peeked through his paws, only to see a thick forest of human legs.

There's no escape! I'm surrounded! he thought, grimly, as his eyes darted from side to side through gaps in the leg-forest.

A rising panic curdled in his tummy at the sound of the News announcement, which blasted out in unison from every TV set. Spinning himself back around to face the window, he was confronted with the following headline:

SELECTION PROCESS COMPLETE FOR 'OPERATION SPACE DUMP'. CATSTRONAUT ANNOUNCED!

His heart began to pound, and his jaw dropped as he blinked blankly through the windowpane.

There, upon the screen, surrounded by News station microphones, cameras and TV News crews, stood an instantly recognisable feline figure, looking somewhat bemused but wearing a very smart state-of-the-art space suit.

"Fatface?" said Furballs, disbelievingly.

"Today's top story!" announced the Newsman. "Operation Space Dump is 'GO FOR LAUNCH'!" he said, bellowing out the last three words with a mad grin.

The crowd outside cheered.

"After a rigorous selection process, a catstronaut has been chosen," he continued, "and he is here today with us 'live'!"

He emphasised the final word with a deep bellow.

FATFACE & FURBALLS' VERY BAD FURDAY

The camera zoomed clumsily in upon Fatface, and in perfect synchrony the array of microphones encircling him instantly swung over, aiming themselves at his head like a Venus Fly Trap entrapping its dinner.

"So," said the Newsman, speaking long distance via a satellite newsfeed, "tell us about your training ... erm ..."

He paused, then somewhat awkwardly turned to his fellow studio guests, who all happened to be retired astronauts from the original Space Station.

"What was his name again? ..." he whispered, self-consciously.

There followed several awkward moments of mutterings.

"... Oh! Ok! Thanks, Major Tim ..." he said, eventually, and turned back to the camera.

"... Commander ... *Fatface!*"

The crowd outside the TV shop exploded with laughter.

You bunch of cheese-bags! thought Furballs, disdainfully. *That's not his real name! It's the only name he was given ... well, before he was given away.*

With his space helmet tucked proudly and neatly under a front feline paw, Fatface stared out through TV screens worldwide, as well as over the small group of gathered reporters, all of whom had been given special invites to the Press Room at the remote NASSA Catstronaut Training Base, or *CATBASE* as the trainees referred to it.

"Ahem!" he began, through his state-of-the-art NASSA installation standard issue Animal-to-Human Translator. "Well, it's not a proper name, but it was the only name I was given ... well, before I was given *away*, that is ..." he added, with a gentle shrug, unaware that the whole world – including Furballs – was hanging upon his every word.

Not wishing to dwell upon Fatface's past, the Newsman ploughed on with his questions.

"Ahem! ... Well, tell us, then, Commander, a little bit more about the space station?"

"Oh," said Fatface, earnestly, "you mean, the International Sewerage Tank in Space Container?"

"That's right, I-STINC," confirmed the Newsman.

The film crew and guest astronauts giggled behind their hands, emitting a few involuntary snorts. Realising what he'd said, the Newsman coughed forcefully to regain his composure, and continued with his questions.

"For example, how far up is it?"

"A long way!" replied Fatface, proudly.

The crowd outside the TV shop chortled amiably while Furballs merely held his head in his paws, and groaned.

Oh, Fatface! The FACTS! They just want the facts!

"Well, they tell me that I'll be able to see the entire planet every hundred minutes or so ..." continued an unflustered Fatface.

"... Oh, wait! ..." he said, suddenly appearing slightly confused. "... Or is it that the planet will be able to see *me* every hundred minutes? And I think they said that everyone will be 400 kilometres below me ... or is it me that will be 400 kilometres above everyone?"

Fatface scratched his head with his free paw.

"I guess it doesn't really matter which way 'round!"

The crowd chuckled.

They're laughin' at yooz Fatface, not with yooz! thought Furballs, with a disgruntled, low growl. *They're just laughin' at yooz ...*

"But it wasn't that hard to get chosen for this mission really," continued Fatface, brightening up. "I mean, the other candidates were so nice and friendly, and they even let me win most of the tests."

The picture switched back to the Newsman.

"Why do you think they did that?" he enquired, earnestly.

"Well," said Fatface, thoughtfully, "I guess they all just really wanted me to be the one to go into Space and represent my planet! I'm very honoured that they let me win, and that I was chosen ..." he added, modestly.

Back at the TV shop, Furballs shook his head.

No! he thought. *There's something seriously not right about this!*

"I see," continued the Newsman, nodding agreeably. "So, finally," he concluded, "Commander Fatface, tell us ... how does it feel to be going into space, knowing the whole world depends upon *you* to successfully complete this historic mission ... on top of a big, explosive ... oops, sorry! ... I mean ... ex-*pensive* rocket ..."

He coughed, awkwardly.

"... I mean ... well, you know, without messing it up?"

Outside the TV shop, the crowd applauded their humble hero-to-be catstronaut as the TV camera shakily zoomed in and out upon Fatface, making everyone feel a bit seasick, whilst in the midst of all this hoo-ha Furballs dragged his paws defeatedly down over his face, leaving a look of disbelief and horror in their place.

No! That's not right! he thought, as he stared at the big TV screen. *You don't know Fatface like I do! He's never wanted to go into space! He's never been brave! Those other trainee catstronauts must have tricked him!*

114

They must have known something that he didn't ... Oh, man! And if I hadn't made him touch that plasma ball-ee thingy ...

The crowd closed in around him.

"... But you see," continued Fatface, now visible simultaneously on every TV screen, (the cameraman had finally managed to keep the camera still), "... I'm not really very brave. You see, I once had a friend ..."

Furballs sprang up onto his hind legs, plonking both front paws suction-pad-like onto the shop windowpane. A great hush descended upon the crowd, and it seemed the entire city had now gathered around the shop window.

"... And, well ..." continued Fatface, lowering his head, his giant image seemingly taking over the entire shop, "... well, I must have done something wrong because he ... hmmm ... he ... ummm ... escaped from The Shelter ... and ... well, he didn't take me with him ... so I guess he didn't want to be my friend anymore."

"NO!!" barked Furballs, despairingly, as his front paws slid listlessly down the thick glass. "That's not *true* Fatface! That's not why I left!"

The gathered crowd began to laugh and mock him.

"Hey! Bozos!" he snapped angrily back at them as he spun around. "Quit your noise! You don't understand! He's my *FRIEND!*"

"Oh look!" said a woman. "The cute little doggy is agreeing with us!"

"Noze I *AIN'T*, lady!" he growled back.

He shook his head and turned back to the window.

What's the use talking to **them***?* he grumbled.

"... And well, I don't really have any other friends ..." continued Fatface, as the cameraman drew right in for a tight close-up. "... So, I guess that means there's no one to worry about me ..."

He lowered his head.

"... you know ..." he said, softly, "... like if somehow I don't make it back ..."

This was too much for Furballs.

"No! Fatface! You got it all wrong!" he barked, as he bounded agitatedly around in little circles. "You gotta come back! *I* need you to come back! I don't got no one else in this world!"

"Oh, look!" said another woman, "the cute little doggy is talking to the catstronaut!"

The crowd began to laugh, hysterically.

"Stop making that stupid noise!" barked Furballs, facing his accusers.

"Oh look!" said a man. "Now he's talking to *us!*"

"Yes!" said someone else. "And he's doing a little dance too!"

Back on the TV screen, the Newsman concluded his interview.

"Well, you're a very brave catstronaut, Commander Fatface!" he said. Then, with a final touch, he added, "And we all wish you the very best of luck!" before abruptly swinging around to face a different camera. "And now," he announced, "our daily repeat episode of 'The Complete History of The World's Presidents'."

FATFACE & FURBALLS' VERY BAD FURDAY

Fatface, still on the podium at CATBASE and unaware that the camera had been switched off, was still thoughtfully considering his reply.

"... Well, actually I'm really not very brave," he said, directly into the blank camera. "You see, my friend – you know, the one I was telling you about – well, his name is Furballs, and he told me I'm not very brave, and although I didn't like hearing it, I realise now that he was right. And I miss him lots. And besides, I'm not even really a cat ..."

However, by now, the reporters had disappeared, and the camera crew had all but packed away their equipment, leaving Fatface standing on the little podium, miles from civilization and his one friend, alone.

Back at the shop, the TV screens had switched back to their myriad conversations, and the laughter had subsided as gradually everyone had drifted off until the only one left sitting there was Furballs.

Oh, geeeezzz, what I am gonna DO? he wailed, as he slumped disconsolately down the shop window onto his bottom.

Some way behind him, a small TV set in the corner of the shop had been broadcasting a separate News item that had just come in regarding a small object that had been spotted in Outer Space by amateur astronomers, who had each expressed extreme confusion due to the fact that this object looked exactly like the dwarf planet Pluto, yet was not in its proper orbit but had strangely been seen 'hiding' somewhere in the Asteroid Belt.

Professional experts had been brought in, including world renowned Quantum Particular Physicists, such as Dr. Jonah Mons, who all shared completely different opinions and had started to argue with each other during the live News broadcast to the point where threats of "I will ruin your career!" had been made against each other.

The item then concluded with a report that the mystery 'Pluto' object had once again vanished, after which the switchboard lit up with viewers calling in to demand the resignation of the current President over this *'Pluto scandal'*, to which the President readily agreed, as it was nearly Saturday and time to swap anyway.

*

It was now late afternoon in the High Street. The shops were closing, and the shoppers had all but departed. Twilight brought its long shadows and damp scent, and although the town was now almost empty, one solitary figure remained outside the TV shop where one television set had been left on, talking to itself and anyone who happened to be passing by overnight in the otherwise silent street.

Although Furballs *knew* he'd done all he could, he nonetheless *felt* that it wasn't enough. Reluctantly, he decided it was time to go and find somewhere to bed down for the night, with the thought that perhaps some inspiration might come to him before morning.

He slowly picked himself up and turned, despondently, to face the shop window, only to see a typed, silent message being looped along the bottom of the solitary TV screen:

"Two days to launch! Brave Catstronaut Commander Fatface to undertake one-way mission to space station I-STINC and unjam the jammed Poop Bay Door!"

Two words struck him.

One-way? thought Furballs.

A pang of dread filled his tummy.

One-way?

The words grew bigger and bigger until they almost made his head burst.

ONE-WAY?!! I knew something didn't feel right about this!

Discordant thoughts tumbled through his mind.

Aren't they going to bring him back? Does Fatface know? I've got to warn him! Floating fleabags, I gotta think this through!

Night was drawing rapidly in, and Furballs decided he best leave the town straight away and find some quiet place to think. And after wandering up and down a few neighbouring streets, he eventually found himself venturing out into open countryside.

Feeling the cool night air upon his face, he stopped to look up at the night sky. A mixture of wonder and dread filled him as he thought about the cold emptiness of Outer Space, and how it seemed to go on forever.

There was also something incredibly beautiful about it too, though, and Furballs found himself getting lost in its endless wonder as he sat there all alone by the empty roadside, surrounded by rustling fields of long grasses.

Where do Time-Travelling Dudey Guys go? he wondered, longingly, as he arced his head around the overhead star-filled sky.

A particularly bright object caught his eye, moving serenely across the backdrop of glittering distant stars, its solar panels glinting with reflected light from the Sun.

It was the I-STINC space station – indeed, the very one that in less than two days would be visited by a small animal from Earth named Fatface; an unimportant, homeless dog, currently wearing a catsuit, whose only wish was to find a real home and have a proper name.

I-STINC indeed! mused Furballs, darkly, as the glimmering space station sped onward in its orbit and faded into Earth's shadow.

No use hiding! I knowz you're still there! he warned.

He began to think hard about how he might find the Time Traveller. Yet, all he could focus upon was finding his friend.

Oh, Fatface! he lamented, as he pondered the Universe. *Maybe yooz already know this is a one-way gig. But I can't bear to think of that. Don't you realise those other cats only let you win because they somehow knew it was a one-way ticket? I know how cats think. They're mean, and think mostly of themselves.*

He sighed, grimly.

I know. I was one.

Something struck Furballs as he stood there beneath the Milky Way. It occurred to him that if Fatface *did* indeed know this was a one-way ticket and yet was going to go anyway, this would, in fact, imply that Fatface would have thought about what that means.

Well, my good buddy, I owes you a big apology. You really are the bravest friend I've ever had.

He gazed upward at the shimmering starlight.

"And yeah, I knowz you're the *only* friend I've ever had," he concluded, soberly and out loud to the starlit emptiness above.

And with that, he laid himself down in the long grass and fell into a restless sleep.

CHAPTER 9 – THE NATIONAL LITTERY CONTEST – PART 1

Furballs' eyes shot open just as a car zoomed past and swerved around the nearby corner. Lying motionless on his back by the grass verge, front paws tucked neatly upon his chest in 'begging' position while his back legs stretched ungainly out into the road, he blinked several times before swiftly retracting his legs at the sound of another approaching vehicle.

The sky was bright and blue, and the Sun was already halfway up its morning climb.

Oh, crumbling catnip! I've overlaid! he groaned. *This would never have happened at The Shelter. Up at dawn, out in The Yard for the 'daily', then back to watch Born Free for the umpteenth time on the Picture Box.*

Oh well, he mused. *I guess I really **am** free now. Mmm, although freedom certainly has a distinctiful chill factor! Brrrrrrrrr!*

FATFACE & FURBALLS' VERY BAD FURDAY

Keeping his head low, he jumped up onto all fours and made a stealthy circle in the grass until he was sure he was alone.

No fancy litter trays out here! Guess I'll have to do it the old-fashioned way. Ah well, at least I got some privacy, for a change.

He proceeded with his daily toilet, and when he'd finished, he turned his thoughts to the memory of the events of the previous day, and to the task ahead.

I either gotta find the Time-Travelling Dudey Guy, or I gotta find Fatface and warn him.

He began to walk along the road, dodging passing vehicles by hopping back into the grass whenever one neared. The recent lorry experience had not enhanced Furballs' estimation of the intelligence of these metal beasts, but he was not in the mood for battle this morning. Plus, he still ran the risk of being seen, reported, and then recaptured.

He wasn't quite sure where exactly he was going, but something inside seemed to be telling him that he would not find his answer back in the city.

Ok, Furballs, think!

He decided to ask himself some questions.

First question: So where do Time-Travelling Dudey-Guys hang out?

Answer: Don't know.

Second question: Where is this NASSA place anyhows?

Answer: Don't know.

He groaned, inwardly.

Think Furballs, THINK!

The wind had begun to bluster, and he found himself struggling against it whilst dodging errant bits of human rubbish.

Out of nowhere, a particularly large piece of paper came flying through the air and landed flat across his face, causing him to stop in his tracks.

*What the furry fluff-balls is **this**? Get off my face!*

He struggled momentarily with the marauding sheet, which somehow didn't want to be ignored. And when he'd managed to remove it clumsily with his paws, he flattened it out upon the ground.

NATIONAL LITTERY CONTEST!
Part of the
National
SCRUFFS ACADEMY
Annual Feline Talent Contest!
Where cats compete against each other to
show who's got the best litter tray!
This year's top prize ...
A trip to Outer Space!
(& Back)

Runner-up prize – a lifetime supply of kitty litter!

*What **is** this?* he mused, twitching his nose curiously as he sniffed the ink for clues.

It was a poster.

Mmm, I've seen this show on the Picture Box, thought Furballs. *And you'd never get me lowering myself to enter something this stupid! ... NEVER!*

He read on.

'This year's top prize – a trip to Outer Space!' it declared, and in much smaller letters, **'(& Back)!'** somewhat unconvincingly.

Furballs suddenly felt a bit dizzy.

*A trip to **outer space**? And **back**?*

His thoughts whirred and fizzed in a blur. He glanced up at the vast expanse of blue sky, knowing that's *exactly* where Fatface would be going, and possibly not coming back from. As the wheels and cogs of Furballs' mind turned, they began to connect into a very unsettling conclusion.

If I could get up there, I might be able to bring Fatface back with me.

He looked down at the poster again, and shook his head.

No, Furballs! NO WAY! There's NO WAY you're even gonna THINK about entering that stupid contest ... all those felines pretending to like each other but would scratch each other's eyes out just to win. And those stupid, STOOPID litter trays, with their fancy PINK bows, BAUBLES and DECORATIONS! It's an insult to any true feline's integrity. It's just ...

His thoughts gathered momentum.

... It's just ... plain ... WRONG!

Another thought flashed into his mind.

Oh, wait! Yes! That's it! Hey, I don't got to enter this stupid contest after all!

A brief moment of relief washed through him.

I just remembered ... I'm the wrong species! I almost forgot I'm currently wearing this pooch-suit! That means ... I'm off the hook! Yay!

However, the relief was short-lived.

Yeah, Furballs, he replied to himself, *but what other available options do yooz currently have?*

The answer was already waiting.

None.

He hoped some sudden inspiration might offer a somehow less dreadful prospect than what appeared to be looming before him, but none came.

He gave the poster one last inspection, which declared, enthusiastically:

'Runner-up prize – a lifetime supply of kitty litter!'

Oh, that's just great, thought Furballs, with another groan. *What does that even **mean**? Do they give it to you all at once? Where would I put it?*

Visions of himself back at The Shelter, squashed up against the cage bars, his cage filled to the brim with kitty litter, with Burt and Pertwee next door thinking he was Fatface, just filled him with a sickly despair.

Yet, what other choice did he have?

Well, it wasn't much of a life, he muttered, glumly to himself.

So, I mayz as well do this.

He drew in a deep, resigned breath, shrugged, and began to make his way, (albeit somewhat reluctantly), toward SCRUFFS ACADEMY.

FATFACE & FURBALLS' VERY BAD FURDAY

*

It was late in the day when he arrived. Keeping to the shadows and following the unlit pathway around the back of the building to the main entrance, Furballs managed to scuttle past the security guard, undetected, by keeping his head down and weaving in and out of yet another forest of human legs as the audience arrived for tonight's contest.

Once inside, a huge Picture Box, announcing the initial heats of the contest, loomed overhead and greeted him.

"WELCOME TO THE ANNUAL SCRUFFS ACADEMY NATIONAL LITTERY CONTEST!" boomed the human Competition Host with a big, cheesy, (and it must be pointed out – *unconvincing*), grin. "HOW TIDY CAN *YOU* KEEP *YOUR* LITTER TRAY?" he declared, with a smarmy scoff.

Furballs stopped briefly to gaze up at the towering TV screen.

*Where did they get **this** guy from?* he thought, with a shudder.

"CONTESTANTS TRAVEL FROM ALL OVER THE GLOBE JUST TO ENTER THIS ANNUAL CONTEST!" bellowed the host. "OPEN TO ALL FEMALE KITTIES, SPAYED or UNSPAYED! THIS YEAR WE ALSO HAVE A SPECIAL CATEGORY FOR NEUTERED MALES!"

The image zoomed out to an overhead view of the main arena where an unnumbered array of litter trays adorned the central space, equidistant to each other in straight, soldieresque rows, each tray being frantically preened and puffed and decorated in last-minute adjustments by its attendant feline contestant.

Furballs shook his head, wearily.

Oh, the shame of it ... my own species reduced to THIS!

The camera zoomed in on one or two contestants during the final touch-ups of their respective litter trays.

"Here we have Contestant Number 345!" announced the Host. "Hello number 345! Can you spare a moment to talk to the viewers?"

There was a slight delay as the Animal Translator processed the info and translated the question for the benefit of all contestants to understand.

Contestant number 345, a bluey-grey Persian female, had her back to the Host and hadn't heard her number-call, focused as she was with her last-minute adornments, inspecting them closely in a crouching position with her tail stuck straight up in the air behind her, pointing directly at the camera.

She was fiddling with several stray pieces of kitty litter, which she then placed neatly around the edge of a sort of pinky-mauve flower arrangement at the far end of her litter tray. The camera frantically zoomed in and out several times before focusing in directly upon what turned out to be … ahem … not her face.

Aw, sheesh! They got the same camera dudey-guy that Fatface had! thought Furballs, feeling slightly nauseous as he stared at the screen. *I hope this guy knows that ain't one of her eyes,* he added, quietly.

The cat, upon seeing her rear on one of the arena screens, turned and gave the cameraman a severe scowl, accompanied by a display of diamond sharp razer-teeth and a scratchy *hiss* for added effect.

The camera quickly wobbled itself over to the adjacent contestant, a Norwegian Forest female, who had been tending to her own litter tray adornments but had stopped to watch the screen and had begun to laugh hysterically at her Persian neighbour, which only provoked *her*, and in a flash the two cats were locked in battle, each one balancing on hind legs, fangs displayed through drawn-back jaws, with front claws pawing and swiping at whatever was within scratching reach.

Their howls and wails filled the hall, causing the gathered audience to issue a wave of shooshes to the very back seats until the entire arena was silently focused upon the ensuing battle.

"Oh!" blurted the Competition Host, somewhat shamefaced. "We seem to have a slight problem!

Goodness me! Look at *that!* A fight has broken out between two of the contestants!"

With a disappointed shake of his head, and a deflated sigh, Furballs picked himself up and began to make his way into the arena, unnoticed, as all eyes were on the two fighting felines who, having failed to intimidate one another, had resorted to all-out warfare, and were now hurling insults at each other's decorated litter trays.

"Who would want to do their toilet in *that?*" spat the Norwegian Forest contestant. "It looks like a hooman garden – all the wrong colour plants, no privacy to poo or ambush birds from, and absolutely no sense of perfume!"

"Well, at least I've added *some* perfume to my litter tray!" retorted the Persian. "Yours smells like a citrus fruit market mixed with cinnamon, chilli and pepper! Yuuuuucckkk!"

"Well at least I didn't try to bribe the judges with catnip!"

Without warning, the Persian kitty launched herself at the Norwegian, who dodged out of the way at the precise moment that the Persian's claws extended themselves at full stretch as she went hurtling over the Norwegian's head and landed splat onto her litter tray, spraying litter pellets, pom poms and a paperchain of origami miniature cat-shapes into the air.

Without hesitation, the Norwegian sprang back at the Persian but missed and landed plum on all fours smack in the middle of her opponent's litter tray, emitting a plume of litter dust, pellets, pinky-mauve flowers, and a photo of the Persian's grandmother, (who had incidentally won the contest several years running), flying into the air and landing in a scattered mess, at which point the referee intervened and disqualified both contestants, adding a year's ban upon the Norwegian for bad behaviour.

Meanwhile, Furballs had kept himself as much as possible out of sight, and had stealthily made his way toward the registration area.

Oh man! How in rat-droppings' name am I going to pull this off? he thought, as he approached the desk, which was currently being occupied by a rather stern-looking, greying mature Burmese.

"Yeeeeesss?" she said, with a sliding, authoritative, (and slightly suspicious), whine.

"Er, yes, er ..." mumbled Furballs.

"Er, yes, er ... *what?*" replied the feline registrar, sharply.

"I ... er ..."

Oh, come on Furballs! Speak up! What's wrong with you?" he said to himself, irritably.

He had never really felt nervous, except of course whenever Fatface had eaten certain spicy foods, which invariably produced some eye-scorching tail-puffs.

However, right now, all he wanted to do was to run out of there screaming. Yet, for some unknown reason, he found that his feet seemed to be concreted to the ground whilst his eyelids blinked uncontrollably back at the registrar.

"I ... er ... I'd like to enter the contest," he announced, awkwardly.

"I'm sorry," replied the registrar, with an unapologetic smirk, "this competition is only open to ... well ... *felines*. In other words ..."

And with a condescending *hiss*, she spat the final syllable out:

"... CATS!"

Furballs stood there, breathing hard.

"Yeah, about that ..." he offered, shakily. "You see, I know this is gonna sound hard to believe ..."

He coughed rather hoarsely, noticing that a queue had started to form behind him.

"Hey! The lady said it's *CATS* only, wise guy!" came a blunt voice from the back. "And if I'm not mistaken," it continued, "*YOOZ* ain't no cat!"

Furballs kept his head down, and hunched his shoulders in an attempt to hide.

"Oi! We ain't got all day, y'know!" came another disgruntled voice.

"Yes! And look!" said another, rather posh-sounding voice. "Goodness me! He didn't even bring his own litter tray!"

FATFACE & FURBALLS' VERY BAD FURDAY

A flurry of agitated gasps swept through the increasingly restless queue.

The registrar peered over her round-rimmed glasses, eyeing Furballs up and down disapprovingly.

"Well?" she said, with a wizened, ancient whine.

Furballs stretched his neck, rolled his head a couple of times in an attempt to release some tension, (which actually only gave him a sharp pain and made things worse), and opened his mouth to speak, hoping the queue would continue to make enough noise so as not to hear him.

The queue-ees, however, thought otherwise.

"Ssshhhhh!! He's going to speak!" came an insistent voice from within the ranks.

Oh, manicured mandibles! thought Furballs, dismally.

The entire parade fell silent, and rows of paws instantly cupped themselves behind their owners' ears to get a better listen.

"This is gonna be good!" came a know-it-all shout from the back.

Furballs' voice dropped to a whisper, accompanied by a distinctly apologetic tone.

"Like I said, this is gonna sound hard to believe, but well ... I really am a ... er ... um ... arrhhh! ... a ..."

"You'll have to speak up!" urged the registrar, with an intolerant huff.

Furballs swallowed hard.

Here goes!

"I'm a ... 'C' ... 'A' ... 'T'!" he whispered, pronouncing each letter deliberately, yet barely audibly.

I hope she don't ask me to say the whole word!

The registrar, however, had other ideas.

"Remind me what 'C' ... 'A' ... 'T' ... spells again!" she snapped.

Oh, flying flea-circuses! Did she read my mind? ... Ok, lady, yooz did ask!

From the corner of his eye, Furballs noticed the Burmese making a strange kind of paw-signal down at her side, followed by a subtle wink to some far corner of the arena.

141

Furballs scrunched his eyebrow patches, suspiciously. Drawing in a deep breath, he puffed out his chest and declared:

"I'm a CAT!" plainly and proudly for all to hear.

There followed a moment of painful silence as the registrar leered disconcertingly down at him. This was presently broken by a rather gruff, coarse and – not especially friendly – human voice from behind.

"Yeah ... and I'm Elsa the Lioness!" it said, without apology.

Furballs suddenly felt what seemed to be a rough human hand grab the scruff of his neck, and he found himself lurching up into the air, his tail and four paws swinging freely as the floor loomed further and further away beneath him.

It was the Security Man.

A faint, dizzying sensation flooded his being as the man swung him round, dangling him at arm's length like an unwanted bag of rubbish on its way out to the bin.

Ooohhhh! he groaned, pathetically, as he tried not to choke.

"Ok, Tiddles!" said the man, with barbed sarcasm. "Let's get you out of here! You might like to consider a visit to the *psychiatrist,* though, before coming back again!" he added, with a sneer, as he paraded a limp Furballs past the queue of booing and mocking feline faces.

Oh, great ... that's just great ... thought Furballs, defeatedly.

"Bye, *TIDDLES!*" they jeered. "Don't call us! We'll call you!"

Fine by me! he thought, as he found himself flying through the air and a door slamming behind him as he landed on all fours out into the fresh night air.

"Yeah, thanks for nothin' and good riddance!" he bleated back at the firmly locked door.

Well, at least I still got my feline landing gear, he acknowledged, as he brushed himself off.

He sighed at the great expanse of night sky that he once again found himself beneath, and as he looked up at the stars his thoughts turned to Fatface, and a pang of regret tugged at his insides.

Boy, that sarcasm stuff certainly ain't so pleasing to be on the receivables end of!

With a heavy sag, he slumped down onto the ground.

Oh! Man-eating tigers! Where are you, Fatface? Only a few hours left until lift-off, and I don't even got a Talking Picture Box to see it happening! Not that I really wants to anyhows ...

"Hey, good buddy!" he said, aloud to the stars. "I tried! I really tried! Who knows where that Time-Travelling Dudey Guy is! I don't even know how to find this NASSA place. But ..."

"Pssst!" came a sound from behind a nearby bush.

Furballs stopped, and glanced warily about himself.

Guess I must be hearing things ... oh well ...

He turned his head back skyward.

"... But," he resumed, to empty space, "they threw me out of the competi ..."

"PSSSSTT!" came the sound again, this time much louder, and with a sense of urgency.

"... tion," he concluded, albeit somewhat hesitantly.

He brought his gaze back earthward, and swung himself around.

"Hey! If that's any of yooz fleabag felines from *in there,* you can ..."

"Sshhhh!" came the sound again, this time much more impatiently.

"Don't yooz *SHOOOSH* meez!" spat Furballs, darting his head from side to side. "Whoever you are, have the guts to come out and show yourself!"

From behind the nearby bush emerged something soft, fluffy, and very feline.

Furballs' jaw dropped to the ground.

"Aarrgghh ... errr ..." he mumbled, picking his jawbone back up, "you're the ..."

Silhouetted by blue-white starlight, hypnotically waving the softest, silkiest tail he'd ever seen, sat a beautiful bluey-grey Persian female pusscat.

"We don't have much time!" she said, glowingly.

"You're the ..." said Furballs, somewhat speechless, "... the one who got disqualified!"

145

"That's right, Einstein," she replied, with a nonchalant swish of her tail. *"Don't* rub it in!" she added, insistently. "Now, come with me ... and *DON'T* make a sound!"

"Where are we going?" he whispered, as they crept around the outside wall of the main arena.

For the first time in his life, Furballs found he had no problem in obeying a female. He hadn't even minded the sarcasm.

"Ssshhh!" came the reply. "I told you to stay quiet!"

"Sorry," offered Furballs, feeling more than a little out of his depth.

"Sshhh!"

He was about to say 'sorry' again, but sensed he would only receive another rebuke.

A small door at the far end of the arena opened ajar as they approached, allowing a thin shaft of light to escape.

"Password?" came a low, edgy whisper from the other side.

"Catnip!" purred the Persian, softly. "Now open the door and let us in!"

The door swung back, and a bright light flooded the surrounding outside area, spotlighting Furballs, who instantly shielded his eyes with his front paw.

"Oi! Are you gonna mince around out there all night?" came a harsh, no-nonsense female voice from inside.

Furballs opened his eyes to a squint, only to find he was now sitting outside, alone.

"Er ... yeah ... I guess," he replied, somewhat hesitantly, as he twisted his head from side to side to verify his solitary status.

With a shrug and a bound he was inside, whereupon the door was slammed shut behind him. He blinked several times, and as his eyes adjusted to the interior light he became aware of the presence of not just one or two female cats, but possibly ten or so, adorned in a semi-circle before him, all eyeing him up and down and muttering to each other in hushed whispers.

"Hey, ladies!" he said, abruptly. "It's rude to whisper in company!"

The familiar form of the Persian Blue female wafted into his vision.

"Oh! Don't worry! They're not saying anything *bad!*" she said, gently placing her paw upon Furballs' front leg.

"Oh, ok, I guess," he replied, feeling suddenly a bit wobbly.

He edged a sideways, downward glance at the delicate paw that lay gently upon his big, ungainly pooch-foot.

"Oh gosh! I'm sorry!" said the Persian, apologetically, pulling her paw abruptly away. "I don't mean to be too familiar," she added, with a shy smile. "There's just something very *different* about you!"

If only she knew ... lamented Furballs, quietly to himself.

"No!" he replied, hurriedly. "It's ok! Really! It's just that ... er ..."

Shut it, Furballs! Now's not the time! Patience! Patience! Concentrate! Oh, gripes!

"I think I know," interrupted the Persian, gently, before turning to face her team with a graceful *swish* of her tail, the delicately perfumed tip of which brushed against Furballs' nose, sending him into a momentary, dreamy trance.

"Ok, ladies!" she announced. "If *we* can't win this *stupid* competition and get a chance to see the world – albeit from outer space – then we'll do our best to make *him* win!"

She pointed a paw in Furballs' direction.

"We'll show those judges who's the smartest!"

The group emitted a loud, joint 'miaow', which shuddered up Furballs' spine with an instinctive urge:

"MIAOW!" they hollered.

Come on Furballs! They musn't suspect you're one of them!

He tried to resist, but it was no use. From the depths of his being, a caterwaul like no other spiralled up and found freedom, surpassing all the lady cats' howls put together with one tremendous bellow:

"MMEEEEEOOOOOOWWWWWW!!"

In perfect unison, the entire group turned abruptly and silently to face him.

"Sorry?" he offered, weakly, his voice trailing upward in pitch.

"You're a pooch, right?" said one of the lady cats.

"Well ... it's a long story," replied Furballs. "I just really, really miss having a good miaow ... Oh! No! Sorry! Erm ... I meant ... I just wanted to join in with the group, you know, with all you ladies here ...!"

He chuckled, uncomfortably, whilst the host of gathered felines stared suspiciously back at him.

"... Er ... what I really meant to say," he continued, dithering somewhat, "was ... 'woof' ... you know ... woof woof! ..." he woofed, unconvincingly, adding, and with a slight clearing of his throat as he circled a front pooch-foot nonchalantly upon the floor, wishing he'd never said anything, "... me being a bona fide pooch, and all that ..."

"O ... kay," ventured the Persian, uncertainly, breaking the awkward silence and turning to face everyone with a silent expression of 'what was *that?*' upon her face. "Any questions?"

"Yeah! I got a question!" said a blue-eyed Himalayan Long-Hair. "Does this guy have a *name?*"

Furballs felt all eyes swing round upon him.

"Well, it's ..."

Come on Furballs, think of a really cool pooch name!

Rex – no, too muscular sounding.

Max – no, too common.

Duke – no, too royal.

Milo – no, too small.

Winston – no, too bulldog-ish.

Buddy – no, too friendly.

Butch – not friendly enough.

Caesar – no, too Roman.

Harley – no, too tough.

Bear – no, too much fur.

Samson – no, not enough fur.

Oh, burping bird-bottoms Furballs! For goodness' sakes, pick a name – ANY name! These guys are all staring at you like you're some kind of brainless bloodhound!

"My name is ..."

The group leaned forward in unison, bending a collective ear towards the captive stranger.

"My name is ..." he stuttered, with a sharp throat-clearing cough.

The group were – by now – leaning so far forward that Furballs wondered if they might topple over.

"... not really important," he said, at last, hoping they'd let it go.

A disgruntled groan emanated from the ranks.

"Oh, come on!" said a stripey grey-white Scottish Fold with flopped-down ears. "You've *got* to have a name! *Everybody* has a name! Now, do you wee laddie got a name, or do you wee laddie *not* got a name!"

Furballs began to feel rather faint and a bit hot under the collar.

"My name is ..."

"Oh, 'ere we go a-*GAIN!*" groaned an anonymous voice from the back, as the entire feline posse craned their necks to make sure they didn't miss it.

"… My name is …" stuttered Furballs, "… er … is …"

"Oh, for goodness sakes! Spit it out, lad!" said a tan-white British Longhair. "This is getting painful! And it's almost my tea-time!"

"And mah wee toenails have groeerrrn an extra inch since I've been awaitin'!" added the Scot.

"Yeah! And Aahh'm gettin' old juss standin' here!" said a pure-white American Bobtail.

"Ok, OKAY!" asserted Furballs, tetchily. "I *hear* you!" *Here goes …*

"Ready?"

"Oh, how much *longer!*" groaned an Egyptian Mau. "My ancestors could have built another pyramid by now!"

"Just *say* it!" griped an Arctic Curl. "It would take me less time to walk to the North Pole!"

"Okay, okay! I'm just making sure!" he justified.

And before anyone else could complain, he simply said:

"Furballs."

A dull, awkward silence fell upon the gathering. Several felines fluttered their eyelids nervously, and a few embarrassed coughs could be heard from somewhere at the back.

"That's a *name?*" said a diminutive Australian Mist. "I've known kangaroos with better names than that!"

"I *told* those guys out there, and now I'm telling yooz!" spluttered Furballs, defensively. "I'm really a *cat*, and the only name I've ever been given is Furballs!"

The tone of his voice stretched upwards, thinly.

"And to prove it, I *know* what you guys *do* with those matted bits of fur that accumulazzerate in your stomach! I used to do it myself!"

He then turned his back to his audience, sat down upon his haunches and, with a loud huff, folded his front pooch-paws.

A voice penetrated the silence.

"Vell, darrrhhlllllink!" said a long-legged Siberian with a rich accent. "I forrrr vun do not care vot anyvun else eezzz sayink! If *you* belieeeeve *you aahhhrrr* ... vot eez it you sayee? ..."

She emphasised the word:

"... POOOSSS-cat, zen zat is fine wiz *me!"*

Furballs lifted his head tentatively, as the group cheered in agreement and high-fived each other with their front paws.

"You know, we've *all* at some point been disqualified," came the familiar soft voice of the Persian, as she approached him, "and it's always that *Norwegian* excuse of a feline who gets us into trouble! And we've had *enough!* Besides," she concluded, calming her voice, "it will help our cause immensely if you *do* believe you're already one of us!"

Furballs crooked his neck around hesitantly to the line of awaiting felines, who in turn angled their heads toward him in perfect synchrony.

"Ok," he said, finally, with a reluctant shrug, "I'll help you ... *if* it helps me," he added, as he stood up and

155

turned to face everyone. "But, we don't got much in the way of time."

Once again, the Persian laid her paw gently upon his.

"Thank you," she said, lowering her head, humbly.

Furballs nodded somewhat nervously before slapping his other front paw heavily upon hers as she turned to move away, whereupon she immediately glanced down with a stern grimace, first at his pooch-foot, then up squarely and questioningly into his eyes.

Shocked at himself, Furballs pulled his paw away, abruptly.

"Oh! I'm ... erm ... I'm sorry," he said, awkwardly. "I just want to know ... your name."

"Lotty," she said, softly, as she reached out forgivingly and reclaimed his paw, placing it gently back upon hers.

"And I'm ... Furballs," replied Furballs, feeling suddenly unintelligent.

"I already know, silly!" said Lotty, with a dismissive giggle. "Now come, we've got to get you ready!"

Furballs was about to query, *"For what?"*, but decided against doing so, as he now realised he had little choice but to go along with whatever had been cooked up by these felines.

Turning back to face her group, Lotty lifted her paw, and with a surprisingly scratchy, raucous caterwaul, made the jubilant announcement:

"Ok ladies!" she shouted. "Let's get to it! Operation Furballs!"

"Yay!" they all cheered in unison, declaring in an equally coarse and tumultuous battle cry, (and much to Furballs' discomfiture):

"OPERATION FURBALLS!"

An expectant hush fell upon the gathering as the female troupe awaited their captive's approval. Furballs, however, tentatively removed his front pooch-paws from over his ears.

"So, ahem ... pardon me for interpurrupting," he interjected, hesitantly, "but what happens now?"

His voice trailed timidly upward in pitch.

"Oh, don't you worry, honey!" said a sleek, grey Korat. "We're going to take the *very* best care of you!"

Furballs grimaced, unconvinced.

"So, don't you go worrying about a single thing, honey bun!" she concluded, with a sparkle in her eye.

"Oh … ok," he replied, uneasily, as he glanced from side to side in search of a potential escape route.

But before he could utter another word, the entire gang had begun moving in, encircling him until he was completely surrounded by lady cats.

CHAPTER 10 – CATBASE LAUNCH PAD, TRAINING SCHEDULE, AND THE BUTTER INCIDENT

Fatface had enjoyed his pre-spaceflight extra special breakfast, and, amidst last-minute checks from the ground-based scientists at MISSION CONTROL, was readying himself for launch.

"Hey, that breakfast tasted really good!" he said, through the intercom as he lay flat, strapped into his seat inside the small capsule known as CATSULE 1, which was perched with precision like an upside-down ice-cream cone atop the main rocket.

He'd spent the previous evening reviewing his Catstronaut Training Schedule and studying what he'd learned in his brief (but gruelling) training course at CATBASE, and the subsequent tests he'd had to undergo, which all catstronauts must complete successfully:

FATFACE & FURBALLS' VERY BAD FURDAY

1. <u>Pre-spaceflight injection:</u> **Check ☑**

   There had been some initial resistance on Fatface's part to this: ("No buddy, you ain't putting that sharp needly-thing in *there!*"). Thankfully, an alternative location had been found, and he'd been rewarded for his 'bravery' with some cat food ... unfortunately for Fatface.

2. <u>Holding his breath for as long as he could</u> (without fainting or allowing the air to escape out of the side of his mouth / blowing raspberries): **Check ☑** (There had been a few squeaks, but it was 'within limits').

3. <u>Jumping from a great height.</u> (Well, it turned out those spindly little stick-like cat legs were useful for something): **Check ☑**

4. <u>Learning the controls of I-STINC via a ground-based 'mock-up'.</u> (Kept getting the sequence mixed up, but succeeded after several long additional hours going well into the evening and way past dinner time, which didn't go down too

well with Fatface, although he was given an extra helping of 'pudding' later – more cat food, but with some icing on top – "Yuk!"). **Check ☑**

5. <u>Final test:</u> One of the instructors was to throw a bone up into the air, (as a symbol of evolution from 'Primitive Survivor' to 'Modern Space Explorer'), which Fatface had to catch in his mouth as it descended without dropping it. (Despite the apparent 'disadvantage' of being a 'cat', Fatface used his natural canine instincts to leap up and *pro-actively* catch the bone mid-air, a fact that was noted by his instructor as 'COMMENDABLE'. Obviously, Fatface kept *very* quiet about his true *canine* status). **Check ☑**

It is a well-known fact that most human astronauts don't go through anywhere *near* as much rigorous, advanced space-travel training as this over the course of several months, or even years, (plus they're not very good at the 'bone catching' exercise). So, to do so in such short amount of time, (one afternoon, in fact), was a real feat of endeavour, and for which Fatface received the highest accolade: a tasty sausage which, *this* time, he was quite happy about.

He checked his list one final time, just to make sure he'd done it all properly, and that all was in accordance with correct procedures.

Having double-checked his list, his little intercom began to bleep:

"Now, Commander," said the man at OPPS Control, "we'll get you comfy in the Command Module, and then we'll go over your Rendezvous, Docking, EVA, and Poop Bay Door Unsticking Procedure one final time. Then, we'll be all set for launch."

"Oh, ok!" replied Fatface.

"Erm, you mean *'copy that'*, don't you?" came another, slightly perturbed voice from the Catsule Communicator, or Catcom, at the Flight Operations Centre.

"Yeah, that's right! *Copy that!*" exclaimed Fatface, uncertainly.

"No worries," came the cool reply. "The main thing is your Communications Carrier Assembly is working ok."

"Come again? Er ... I mean ... copy that?"

"Your Snoopy Cap, Commander ... you know ... the thing you're wearing on your head so that we can talk to you?"

"Oh! Yes! I mean ... copy that! My Commonooomicaticoms Carrying Assembling thing! I call it the Snoopy Poopy Cap! But, yeah! Gotcha! I mean ... copy that!"

"We hear ya, loud and clear, Commander," replied the Catcom, smoothly. "We're just making final checks on the transfer lines of the orbiter's manoeuvring and reaction control system, and making a few final checks that they are stowed safely on board your capsule."

"Copy that!" replied Fatface, robotically, though somewhat uneasily. "Can I ask a question?"

"You mean, you have *some words* for us, Commander?" replied the Catcom.

"Oh!" gushed Fatface. "Yeah! I mean ... I have ..."

He cleared his throat.

"... Ahem!"

A howl of feedback whistled around inside the capsule, and some vague expressions of pain could be heard through the intercom from Mission Control.

"No need to shout, Commander!" replied the Catcom, with a nervous laugh.

"Sorry!" said Fatface, whispering, *"copy that ..."* just to make sure he was following correct procedures. "Oh yes! I ... erm ... oh, what was it I wanted to say?"

"You have some words for us?"

"Oh yes!"

"Please go ahead, Commander. Take your time ... but not *too* much, as we're about to launch!" added the Catcom, with another nervous chortle.

"It's ok!" whispered Fatface. "I remember now."

"Just talk at normal volume, Commander!"

"Oh ... yeah, ok!"

He cleared his throat, rather coarsely amidst another howl of feedback.

"Ahhhhem! It's about that MONOMETHIC HYDRO-THINGY that you said was on board my spaceship ..."

A stony silence filled the capsule.

"... Well," he continued, unabated, "it sounds a bit ... well ... you know ... kind of ... *explody*."

"Copy that, Commander," replied the Catcom, "and we have some words for you. By 'explody', do you mean, can the monomethyl hydrazine fuel and the nitrogen tetroxide oxidizer potentially ignite?"

"Er... yeah, that," replied Fatface, uncertainly, adding, "do we always have to say, 'we have some words'?"

"Well," replied the Catcom, "we have some words about that too, but to answer your first query ... oh, hold on Commander, the Flight Director wants to say something ..."

"Good morning, Commander Fatface!" came an authoritative female voice over the intercom.

"Oh! Erm ... copy that!" replied Fatface.

"I have some words for you," said the Flight Director.

"Yeah, I thought you might say that," replied Fatface, feeling very sure of himself, adding, "copy that!" just to sound professional.

"We're very proud of you, Commander Fatface," continued the Director, "and we know you'll have a good flight."

"Thank you ... copy that ... Oh! I mean, copy that, and thank you," said Fatface, getting himself all confuddled.

"Oh, and one more thing," said the Director, "although the monomethyl hydrazine fuel and the nitrogen tetroxide oxidizer is extremely flammable, these hypergolic fluids are stored in well-separated areas on the southwest and southeast corners of the Command Module, respectively. Transfer lines convey the fluids through the fixed service structure to the hypergolic umbilical system located on the rotating service structure, with its three pairs of umbilicals attaching to the orbiter."

There followed a long pause.

"So, then ..." replied Fatface, in a sort of wobbly whisper, "... it won't explode?"

"Well, hopefully not very much," replied the Director, adding a hurried, "have a good flight!" before disappearing off.

"Copy that," said Fatface after a long pause, having begun to feel rather weak.

The Catcom's voice resumed over the intercom.

"Now remember, Commander, we won't say the number 'five' during the countdown as it sounds too much like, 'FIRE'!"

The Catcom pronounced the last word somewhat abruptly.

"Oh!" replied Fatface, as he jumped in his seat.

"I'm sorry, Commander," chuckled the Catcom, "I was just having a bit of fun with you there! There's no real fire! We're just saying we *won't* say that number in case you think there *is* a fire and hit the ABORT button!"

Fatface gently lifted his hovering paw away from the big red button with the word 'ABORT' in large letters above.

"Oh ... erm ... copy that," he replied, feebly.

A more urgent situation had, in the meantime, reared up in Fatface's mind. Or, more accurately, in his bladder.

"I have some words for you," he said, delicately.

"Copy that, Commander, go ahead, we're listening," replied the Catcom.

"Request permission to use The Tray," said Fatface, in a slightly strained tone.

"Oh … erm … copy that, I think," came the Catcom's equally hesitant reply.

Some muffled sounds could be heard as if the Catcom were covering his microphone with his hand whilst talking to someone else.

"Ahem! Request permission to use the Tray!" repeated Fatface, somewhat urgently. "Hey guys! Can anyone hear me? I gotta take a leak!"

"We hear you!" replied the Catcom. "We just didn't plan for this!"

"Hey! I've been sittin' up here for hours! And you guys didn't think of that?"

Fatface found himself somewhat surprised at his sudden assertiveness.

"We're very sorry about that, Commander," said the Catcom, sheepishly. "Can you hold on for just a bit longer while we find a solution?"

"I guess," said Fatface, reluctantly. "But to me, the only solution is to do what nature's telling me very loudly to do!"

"Copy that, Commander, just hold on!" added the Catcom, hurriedly.

Oh, boy! thought Fatface, as he rocked himself uncomfortably back and forth in his seat. *What can I do to take my mind off **this**?*

Several moments later, a voice came back in Fatface's Snoopy Cap:

"Commander, can you hear me?"

There came no reply.

"What's that noise? Commander, is that you?"

A faint humming of the same three notes could be heard over the intercom, and was now filtering down through the Control Room at Mission Control over the public address system, with occasional bursts in volume followed by subsequent lulls.

"Mmmmm ... mmm ... **MMM**mmm ... mmm**MMM!!** ..."

It seemed to be going round in a cycle, which would then repeat itself from the beginning with increased urgency.

"Er ... is that *you,* Commander?"

"Mmmm ... **MMMMM** ... mmmmm ... **MMMMM!**"

"Well, I guess we'll just have to take that as a 'yes'," said the Catcom. "I've had a word with the Flight Surgeon ..."

"Mmmmm ... **MMMMmmmm!**"

"And he says it would be too dangerous ..."

"MMMmmmMMM ... **MMMMmmm!!**"

"... to allow the ... ahem ... *liquid* to enter your space suit, as it might create a ..."

"Mmm ... **MMMMmmm!!!**"

"... short circuit and short out the controls. Commander?"

"Mmmm ... **MMMmmm** ... **mmmMMM!!!**"

"... Oh! ... I've just heard from the Flight Director. She's overruled the Flight Surgeon, and said you may now ... well ... use the 'Tray' as you call it. She says if only to stop the humming ... in other words, you have permission to relieve yourself in your space suit!"

The intercom went abruptly silent at both ends.

"Commander? Are you there?"

A new sound began to filter down through the speakers at Mission Control.

"Aaaahhhhhhhhhhh! ..." it went, on and on, "... Oooooooooooo ... aaaahhhhhhh ..." and finally, "... OH YEAH, BABY!"

"Commander?"

Some awkward coughing noises spluttered across the intercom from the capsule before a familiar voice resumed.

"Copy thaaaaaaaat!" said Fatface, with a smooth swagger. "Ahhh, that feels so much better!"

"Good to have you back with us, Commander!" said the Catcom. "Flight Surgeon says readings are a little ... well ... *saturated*, and some of the warning-lights are flashing red, but you're still within limits, and nothing's shorted out ... yet. So, are we good to go now?"

"You bet!" said Fatface, casually. "I'm a wet bag alright, but I'm cooler than you! So, let's LIGHT THIS CANDLE!"

A few cheers could be heard over the intercom from Mission Control, followed by some abrupt 'shooshing' sounds.

"Oh, and by the way, Commander," came the Catcom, "can you confirm you have the Oil-Can stowed safely? You'll need this to unstick I-STINC's jammed Poop Bay Door."

Fatface stared down at the little pot of oil, with its small, purposely adapted spout which had been attached to the floor, (just so that it didn't start to float about).

"Copy that, Ground Control, it's here!" he replied, affirmatively.

"Ok, Commander, copy that. Finally, we just want to say we've also included a little treat for you!"

Fatface looked about himself, eagerly.

"We understand you're quite partial to butter, so we've stashed a bar of it in the rear of the capsule, where it's cold so that it won't melt!"

"Oh, er ... copy that," replied Fatface, somewhat reticently.

The sudden reminder of the memory of the *'butter episode'* still plagued Fatface, even after all this time since that fateful day when the Shelter Lady had left a whole bar of it out in the kitchen, and Fatface, seeing *Cage Number 6's* open door, had scampered through undetected and had followed his nose straight to that slab of butter, eating the whole thing in one go.

FATFACE & FURBALLS' VERY BAD FURDAY

Needless to say, punishment and humiliation had ensued in the form of a soft, mesh muzzle for the night, which only delighted Furballs in reminding Fatface of this traumatic memory at every opportunity since.

However, the trauma had not lessened Fatface's fondness for the creamy offering, and something within him softened at the thought that the guys at NASSA had been that thoughtful.

"Thanks, that's really nice of you," he said, adding, "I think I'll save it for when I've opened I-STINC's door and performed OPERATION SPACE DUMP, and then I can relax a bit."

"You're welcome, Commander!" came the reply.

A final pre-flight thought came to him.

"Hey guys," he said, casually, "just before I leave, can you just remind me what *'E' 'V' 'A'* stands for again?"

"Oh - kay, Commander," came a slightly nervous voice over the intercom. "But ... well ... we have *already* gone over this *several* times today. And we're just about to launch!"

"Oh, I was just teasing you!" lied Fatface, with a slightly edgy laugh.

"Ok, Commander. Initiating Launch Sequence. Commencing Countdown, engines on."

"Copy that," acknowledged Fatface, feeling more professional by the minute. "And, oh, by the way," he added, "what number does the Countdown start on again?"

A brief whistle howled over the radio, which then fell deadly silent.

"Hello?"

Silence.

"Oh well, I guess that's *meant* to happen," he said aloud to himself, turning his thoughts to his question.

"E ... V ... A ..." he pondered. "Oh ... what was it again? Arrgghh! ..."

A mechanical female voice filtered into the capsule.

"Ten ... nine ... eight ..."

"Oh! I know! I know!" he announced, as he bounced around in his pilot seat all excitedly.

"... seven ... six ..."

A faint rumble began to shake the seat, and everything began to rattle and jiggle about.

"E ... V ... A ..." he said, judderingly, as the growling rumble boomed up through the rocket.

RRRRRrrrrrrruuummmmble!!!!

"Extra ... Vet ... no, er ... Extra ... Vum ..."

Ruuuuuummmmble! Roooooooaaaaarrrrrr!

"... four ... three ..."

"Extra ... oooh ... er ... Venticular! ... no! That's not it!"

Whooooooooshhh! Ju-dddddddder!

"... two ..."

"Oooooo! I ger ... ger ... got it!" he warbled, as his seat began to shake uncontrollably.

"... ONE!"

"Extra ... Vehicular ... Activity!" he bellowed, triumphantly, as he felt himself begin to move slowly upwards.

"Commander!" came a voice over the intercom. "We lost you back there briefly, but we're reading you loud and clear again!"

"Th ... th ... th ... thanks!" stuttered Fatface, as he gripped the sides of his pilot seat. "Is th ... th ... this thing moving?"

Amidst the din of the rocket, some faint chortles could be heard from Ground Control.

"Oh, ha ha, Commander! We appreciate the joke!" said the Catcom.

"No! I'm sss ... sss ... serious!" replied Fatface, his front paw-knuckles turning white from gripping the seat.

"Well," came the Catcom's voice, "you *do* have several million pounds of thrust beneath you!"

"Is th ... th ... th ... that good?" juddered Fatface.

"Well, it's ..."

The Catcom paused.

"... Yes, Commander, it's good," he said, eventually, as if he didn't want to mention the big ball of fire that was coming out of the base of the main rocket. "We're just about to go into radio-silence now."

"I'd ra ... ra ... ra ... ather ... yer ... yer .... you di .... di ... di ... didn't!" offered Fatface, feeling his lips suddenly go all wobbly and some invisible force pull his ears and whiskers back behind his head.

"You won't be able to talk to us," concluded the Catcom. "And we won't be able to hear you scream ... oops, sorry, we're just kidding about that! Can you confirm you're ok to go?"

"I'm...mm...mmm...oh...k...k...kay...t...t...t...to...g ...g...g...go!" warbled Fatface, trying to keep his face in one position, yet finding his cheeks and lips quivering all over the place.

"Ok, see you downstream."

The voice stopped abruptly, and all that could be heard beneath the roar of the rocket was an unfriendly 'hiss' in Fatface's Snoopy Poopy Cap.

His training at CATBASE had been brief but thorough, (due to the urgency of the I-STINC situation), and he recalled there had been something mentioned along the way about what happens during launch, and that it was going to be a little uncomfortable. However, he'd tuned out during that part of the training due to it being nearly lunchtime and his tummy was rumbling rather loudly, (so much so that the instructor had had to raise his voice above the noise).

Consequently, back in CATSULE 1, Fatface now wished he'd listened a bit more to the instructor and less so to his growling stomach. Yet, despite this, as the rocket began to move upwards faster and faster, it didn't actually *feel* as bad as he'd imagined, except if he went to turn his head even slighty, he found that ... well ... he couldn't ... and that it would probably be best to shut his mouth if only he could keep his lips from wobbling about all over the place.

What was that thing called? I know it had a weird, funny kind of name, some 'Gs' with a number, he thought, in between closing one side of his mouth, only for the other to flap open and wobble uncontrollably.

It was only then that he remembered they weren't even *his* lips, but were in fact Furballs'.

Hey, buddy! he thought, *I don't know where you are. I hope you're ok. I'm sorry about whatever I did that made you go away. I guess you were right about me. I'm really not that smart, or brave, and I don't really understand all the stuff these clever hoomans have got me doing here. But anyways, I'll take care of your catsuit ... if I ever make it back to The Shelter.*

Suddenly, the roar of the rocket and the shaking and rattling and juddering of the capsule didn't seem to matter as much. Struggling against the invisible nameless force, Fatface managed to turn his head ever so slightly toward the small triangular window, out of which all he could see was a deepening blue.

The invisible force began to lessen, and to his delight Fatface found that his ears and whiskers had not been blown away, and were still happily attached to his head and face, as too were his lips, which he now stretched into an 'ooo', then and 'ahhh' shape, just to check they were still in the right place and were usable. Nonetheless, his entire being felt a little, well, *numb*.

The deep blue of the outside sky had now turned several shades darker until, all at once, it became the clearest, deepest, emptiest black Fatface had ever seen.

He blinked several times, as there was something else there too, and he wanted to make sure it wasn't just an after-effect of the rocket launch.

He'd seen these little points of light back when he was out on the streets as a young pup, all alone. His mother, who had been quite old when she had him, had soon afterward 'gone to the Eternal Yard', or so he'd since been informed by Burt, and which explained why Fatface had been left completely alone at such a young and delicate age.

He remembers having looked up into the vast sky and seeing all those little twinkly things looking back down at him. He didn't know why, but somehow this had comforted him, and even though it was shortly after that that he was captured, along with Furballs, he nonetheless held onto this memory, and whenever he felt afraid, he would think about those twinkly lights shining down upon him, protecting him, and telling him he was safe.

"Commander?"

A faint voice penetrated his thoughts.

"Commander Fatface?"

"Yep!" he replied, slightly startled. "Oh! I mean, *copy that!*"

"Good to hear you! We thought you'd passed out!"

"No! I was just ... well, I was just thinking of someone."

"Welcome to Space, Commander!" exclaimed the Catcom, jubilantly. "Please verify position and trajectory."

"Well, erm ... I seem to have stopped."

"Come again?"

Fatface unstrapped his seatbelt to get a better look out of the little window.

"Wooaahh!"

"Please clarify!" requested the Catcom.

"Wooahh! What's happening?! I'm floating!"

"Er ... yes, Commander," resumed the Catcom. "You were pulling three Gs back there, but now you're in Zero G! Don't you remember your training?"

Kind of, thought Fatface, as the memory of that particular training session came flooding back.

Oh, yes, that warm, sunny afternoon where he'd worn his NASSA standard-issue designer mirrored sunglasses, and, propping himself up on his elbows at his classroom desk, had started to feel his eyelids droop behind his shades, only to open them again at the sound of everyone else leaving the classroom an hour later.

Returning his thoughts to CATSULE 1, he formulated his reply.

"Is *that* why my ears and whiskers were nearly pulled off my head? Three 'Gs'? So, does *Zero G* mean I can keep my ears and whiskers where they're supposed to be?"

"That's affirmative!" said the Catcom.

"Yay! Ok then! Zero G! I'm on it!" said Fatface, as he bounced gently off the capsule's hull, only to head straight into the opposite hull-wall and bounce off *that* one, and then back again several times.

Now where did they put that Zero G thingy ...

"CATSULE 1 to Ground Control," he announced, recalling at least *something* of the official terminology.

"Copy that, go ahead, Commander."

"I'm just searching for that *Zero G* thingy. I can't quite find it, but I'll let you know as soon as I do!"

"Er, thanks Commander, I think ..." came the slightly confused reply. "Just let us know your position and proposed ETA at I-STINC. We can then begin implementation of OPERATION SPACE DUMP."

"Yeah sure, I'll look for those things too!" he added, as he searched frantically around the capsule for anything that might look like a *'Zero G'*.

Several moments later, and having failed to find it, he reached out and grabbed the armrest of the pilot's seat, pulled himself back down into it, and secured his seatbelt.

"Ok, Commander, copy that, and if you could just state your position, that would be a great help!" urged the Catcom.

"Oh! Yes! That's easy! I'm in space!"

"Erm ... thanks Commander. If you could be just a *little* more specific, that would help us greatly!"

"Well, I don't appear to be moving!" shouted Fatface, into his Snoopy Poopy Cap microphone. "I can't find the brake, but I guess I must have stopped because everything outside doesn't seem to be moving!"

"Ok, Commander. Please clarify, when you say *everything outside,* to what are you referring?"

"You know, those little twinkly things that light up the night and make you feel ... well ... that you're not all alone. Except ..."

He paused momentarily, and craned his neck forward to get a better look through the window.

"... they don't seem to be so twinkly up here."

"You're talking about the stars, Commander, and out there in Space there's nothing to get in the way of their light. It's only from the ground that stars seem to twinkle, as the airstreams, winds and dust from the atmosphere make the light appear to wobble."

Given his recent experience during launch with the *invisible force,* which he now understood to be some letter 'Gs' with a 'number 3' in front, Fatface knew *all* about wobbly things. And he didn't care too much to hear that something he couldn't actually *see* from the ground was making his little twinkly lights in the night sky go through the same trauma.

Nonetheless, he was here to complete a mission, and as he frantically searched the array of switches before him, a stream of ever-changing numbers presented themselves on the computer.

"CATSULE 1 to Mission Control. Do you copy?"

"Mission Control to CATSULE 1. Hey Commander, we copy you loud and clear!"

"Good! Because I think there's a problem!"

"Copy that. Please state the nature of the problem."

"Well, um … oh! Sorry … I mean, *copy that* … ahem … basically, all the numbers are jiggling about!"

"Er … copy that," came a somewhat subdued voice from downstream. "So, er … what exactly is the problem, Commander?"

"Well, all these … oh sorry, I meant to say, *copy that* first … all these red numbers and green numbers are jumping around all over the place, but I don't seem to be moving."

"Please clarify! We're reading the same numbers down here, and we can verify that you're moving along at quite a speed!"

"I don't think so … I mean, *copy that,* I don't *think* so! I just seem to be floating around! I mean, I can't feel myself moving!"

"Copy that, Commander, that's because you're in a vacuum, and there's no friction! You're moving, but you won't feel it!"

"Oh," replied Fatface, suddenly feeling a bit weak. "So, I don't have to find that Zero G thingy then?" he said, with a squeak.

"No, Commander! You're already *in* it!"

"Oh!" he replied, scrunching up his eyebrows. "Is that good?"

"You bet that's good, Commander!"

"Oh, well, thank you!"

"You're welcome, Commander!"

Feeling almost-but-not-quite certain of things, Fatface ventured forth the question that was hammering in his head, but which he nonetheless felt somewhat afraid to ask.

"So ... er ... exactly how fast *am* I going, then?"

"Well, Commander, you're orbiting at an average speed of 27,000 kilometres an hour. Would you prefer that in miles per hour?"

There was a slight pause.

"Is it more in miles per hour?" said Fatface, shakily.

"No, no, Commander!" said the Catcom, jovially. "It's the same speed in miles per hour!"

"Oh, ok, don't worry then," said Fatface, gripping the sides of his seat and beginning to regret that large 'special' breakfast he had eaten earlier.

He peered delicately out of his little triangular window. Everything was serene and still.

"CATSULE 1 to Ground Control, are you *sure* I'm going that fast! I'm not even sure I'm *moving!*"

"Ground Control to CATSULE 1, copy that, Commander. Well, there's only one way you can be *really* sure that you're moving!"

Fatface found some words coming out of his mouth that he didn't really feel like saying because the answer coming back might involve hearing something he didn't really want to hear.

"And how's that?"

"If you look out your window, you'll see a big blue round thing."

Fatface craned his neck and stared up out of his little window.

"All I see are the little non-twinkling twinkly lights. Everything else is just black."

"No, no, Commander! You need to look *down,* not *up!*"

He unstrapped himself from his seat, and, gripping onto whatever was within reach, floated over to the window, whereupon he turned his gaze downward.

There, hiding beneath his spacecraft, was the big blue round thing.

"Has *that* been there all the time?" he said, tentatively.

"Well, yes, Commander, it's *home!*"

Home?

The word sent a chill around Fatface's being.

*So **that's** what The Shelter looks like from the outside! Wow! It's prettier than I'd imagined! And rounder!*

"It's prettier than I'd imagined!" he said, echoing his thought aloud as he stared down at the planet beneath him. "And so much *bigger!*"

"It's beautiful, isn't it Commander?" said the Catcom, with a sort of 'a-long-time-ago-I-was-an-astronaut' sigh.

Fatface's thoughts turned to his friend.

*Oh, Furballs! Where **are** you? For that matter, where am **I?***

The planet rotated serenely and silently beneath the spacecraft.

"It seems to be moving *really* slowly!" said Fatface, airing his thoughts as they came. "Are you *sure* I'm the one that's moving?"

"Well, Commander, the planet *and* you are both moving! And remember, there's no *friction* in the vacuum of Space!"

"Oh, I see," lied Fatface, dreamily, as he scratched his head again.

He recalled the word 'friction' from when Furballs would get a good brushing from the Shelter Lady, who would then blow up some balloons, rub them against his fur, and then the balloons would stick to her jumper. She also tried this in reverse, rubbing the balloons on her jumper and then sticking them to Furballs, watching gleefully as he would swipe at them with his paws until they burst.

Furballs then learned pretty quickly that this made a very loud noise, and so whilst he hated having balloons stuck to his fur, he knew the only way to rid himself of them was to get a horrible loud bang. The problem was, he never knew *exactly* when the 'bang' would happen, and so he would spend the rest of the afternoon shaking in the corner. The Shelter Lady always found this amusing.

Fatface also recalled the word 'VACUUM', and didn't think it sounded as frightening as the scientists had warned him it could be. (Part of the training had been:

"DON'T OPEN THE DOOR UNLESS YOU'VE GOT YOUR SPACESUIT ON!", or, more clearly, "PUT YOUR SPACESUIT AND HELMET ON *BEFORE* OPENING THE DOOR!"), as again he recalled the Shelter Lady pushing a noisy machine up and down the corridor once a week, often referring to it as her 'vacuum'.

He didn't really see what all the fuss was about with this so-called *vacuum of space*, and there certainly were no signs of either the Shelter Lady's machine or – for that matter – the Shelter Lady.

Maybe this is where she goes when she's not at The Shelter? pondered Fatface, as he scratched his chin, intelligently.

His thoughts were interrupted by Mission Control.

"Catcom to CATSULE 1, you're about to head into the planet's shadow, and we'll lose contact with you for about an hour. Will you be ok?"

"Well, if there's a Picture Box onboard, I'd quite like to watch a movie!"

"Copy that, Commander! I understand you like the movie, *Born Free?*"

As much as Fatface loved that movie, (and it was his forever favourite movie of all time), without Furballs around to complain about how many times he'd already seen it, it didn't really *feel* right to watch it now. Besides, it would only encourage him to want to go outside and run around – and *that* would mean *OPENING THE DOOR!*

He'd had the foresight to stick a note, (in his best handwriting), upon the capsule door, saying:

'DOeN'T OPpEN ThE DOR!'

So, it seemed better not to encourage doing so.

"CATSULE 1 to Mission Control, thanks, but I think I'll give it a miss for now."

"Copy that, Commander! Well, we suggest you get some rest then. FYI, CATSULE 1 is making a perfect heading toward I-STINC. Your ETA is two hours and thirty-one minutes. Once there, we can begin Rendezvous and Docking Procedures. After that, you're on your own for your EVA and Poop Bay Door

Unsticking Procedure, after which you can perform OPERATION SPACE DUMP. The whole world's depending upon you to succeed! But we're right there with you!"

Somehow, the last sentence didn't really *feel* that way to Fatface as he stared out of his lonely window, first looking up at the non-twinkling twinkly lights, then down at the giant, glowing blue rotating jewel with scrubby little green, brown, and fluffy white bits, its vast areas of the deepest blue, and the thin ghostly veil than delicately encased it all.

Is 'E' 'T' 'A' the same as 'E' 'V' 'A'? he contemplated, thoughtfully, as CATSULE 1 drifted into planet Earth's shadow, and the distant little night-lights from cities far below glowed from the kinds of homes Fatface had never known – homes that offered warm fires to sleep by, catflaps and dogflaps to roam freely through, and a proper name to be known by.

CHAPTER 11 – THE NATIONAL LITTERY CONTEST – PART 2

Furballs sat nervously amidst the host of female cats, who back at SCRUFFS ACADEMY were busy discussing what seemed to him to be some kind of plot, him being the main protagonist, or *prey,* as he quietly noted (somewhat bleakly) to himself.

"By the way, my name's Matilda ... Matty for short!"

A bright, young, smiling blue-cream Turkish Angora stood before him, tape measure in paw.

"Matty?" replied Furballs.

"Yes, my owner is always having to brush me because my fur gets all matted in knots and tangles! Hence, *Matty!"*

"You have a *home?"* he queried. "A real *home?* And a proper name *too?"*

"Yes," replied Matty, shyly. "I'm spoiled rotten! It's wonderful! Especially on my birthday!"

195

Holding one end of the tape measure in her paw, she flung the other around Furballs' neck.

"*Birthday?*" he coughed.

"Sorry, don't mean to strangle you!" she replied, playfully. "Yes! When's *your* birthday?"

Furballs had to think.

"I don't actually remember being born," he replied, uncertainly, while scratching his head.

"Oh no! I didn't mean *that!* I mean, when do you get your special gifts? My hoomans give me treats and prezzies, and it always seems to be on the day when the flowers are all out in the garden and the day is very long! I can tell my birthday is coming because of that, and I get *soooooooooooo* excited!"

The two final words oozed out in a frightful squeal, causing Furballs to block his left ear with his paw.

"Oh, I see, I think ..." he stuttered, whilst rattling his head from side to side, just to check he could still hear.

He paused slightly before meekly concluding, "... Well, no, actually, I don't really see."

He recalled that back at The Shelter every animal who'd been there for a certain length of time would be brought a special meal, which the Shelter Lady called a 'cake', and which had pointy things sticking out of it with little flames on their tips.

'Fire' had never been one of Furballs' favourite subjects, so to see other inmates jumping for joy at this *flaming cake*, as he called it, would merely reinforce his conclusion that he was the only Shelter occupant with all his marbles still intact.

"I guess I must have been born on one of those days … I just don't know which one it was," he admitted, doubtfully. "I don't recall what the weather was doing, and besides, there were no flowers where I used to live. And the doors were shut at the same time every day, so every day was the same length … well, the same *everything,* actually."

He shrugged a helpless shrug.

All I really remember from way back then, he thought, quietly, *is just … well, waking up one day outside in the street, being caught in a net and slung into a small cage with Fatface, and if it weren't for him, I probably would have gone mad – even though he almost drove me mad on a daily basis.*

Without realising, he'd said Fatface's name out loud.

"You mean you actually *know* Commander Fatface?" enquired a slightly starstruck Matty.

"Yeah, well, not anymore ... it's a long story ..."

"I think they already launched ... it was just on TV!" she added, helpfully.

"TV? Oh, you mean the Picture Box? He's *gone?*"

Furballs groaned as his head slumped down onto his chest.

"Oh, man ..."

"Oh, that's so sweet that you still call it the Picture Box!" gushed Matty. "We spoiled kitties have picked up *far* too many words from hoomans! And don't even *start* me on what they call *compooters* and *compooter mouses!*"

"Mice," corrected Furballs, with gloomy indifference.

Not that the young feline was really listening, due to her seemingly inexhaustible excitement about ... well ... almost *everything*.

She giggled mischievously, then seeing Furballs' glum expression sighed and placed a slightly matted paw upon his.

"He's on a special mission to help all of us," she offered, looking up, hopefully, with her bright, turquoise eyes into his. "And they're sending regular reports!" she added, encouragingly.

"That's what I'm afraid of," lamented Furballs, dolefully. "You don't know Fatface like I does!"

"Come on!" she said, grabbing his paw and jumping up. "We've got a contest to win! And *you're* going to win it!" she added, as she dragged him across the room.

*

"So, what the tinned tuna exactly are you going to do with me?" said Furballs, flatly, as they approached the group.

"Well ..." replied Lotty, turning to greet him. Yet, as she did so, something within him melted.

Oh boy! She is BEE-EWW-TIFF-OOLL!

"... We heard you say you're a cat," she continued, "and we also saw that *dreadful* News report about Commander Fatface, and how it seems he's on a one-way trip."

She cleared her throat, as if to prepare for some uncomfortable speech.

"Now," she resumed, boldly, "we don't know *exactly* why you would say you're a cat, but I'm guessing you and Commander Fatface know each other, and *you're* the friend he mentioned in the TV interview ..."

Wow! She's smart! thought Furballs, as he sat blinking at her.

"... Anyhow," she continued, "I noticed that you don't behave the same way most pooches do, and then when I thought about why a *canine* would enter a *cat* contest to go into outer space – and back – it all suddenly made sense!"

She stopped mid-flow, scrunched her eyebrows, and tilted her head to one side.

"Why are you blinking?" she said, bluntly, and with more than a little irritation.

"Erm ... I don't really know!" replied Furballs, as he attempted to keep his eyes wide open, which only made him look *really* weird.

"Well, um, anyway," concluded Lotty, somewhat distractedly, "it seems to me ... well, to all of us ..."

She stopped.

"... Are you *sure* you're ok, Furballs? I mean, what are you *doing* with your eyes?" she enquired, feeling more and more perturbed. "Do you need *The Tray* or something?"

"No!" squawked Furballs, indignantly, yet with a somewhat strained squint. "I'm fine there!"

"It's just that ..." she offered, hesitantly, "... you don't look so good, and your eyes are watering!"

Furballs scrunched up his eyelids, simultaneously letting out a relieved grunt, after which he found himself blinking even more so than he had done to begin with.

"I was actually trying *not* to blink ..." he puffed, feeling more than a little embarrassed, as he rubbed his now-sore eyes with his paws.

"Well," continued Lotty, with a *'I don't know what **that** was all about'* huff, "it seems to me ... in fact to all of us ... that for some reason only *you* know, you want to win this contest and bring back your friend."

She's figured it all out, he silently concluded, adding the afterthought ... *well, not quite **all** of it.*

"Yeah, I guess," he said, casually, "that was the plan. But, anyhows ..."

"Well," she snapped, "*this* is your chance to help your friend!"

"How? By half-strangling me with a tape measure?" he queried.

Lotty's cheeky giggle could be heard from deep within the ranks.

"It's for your catsuit!" she said, eagerly.

"Catsuit?" enquired Furballs, with a sort of upward squeak, as a sudden rather *faint* sensation flooded his being.

You gotta be kidding me! he said to himself.

"Yes!" replied Lotty. "You won't win this contest looking like a canine, so we have to disguise you as a feline ... you know, a *cat!*"

Yeah, I know, thought Furballs, bleakly.

"Oh, and by the way ..." added Lotty, turning abruptly and pointing to somewhere just above his back knees, "... this competition is only open to females and neutered males, so we'll have to do something with *those!*"

With a palpable wince, Furballs shuddered and crossed his back legs.

"Oh ... those aren't mine!" he blurted, immediately regretting the public proclamation.

Lotty glared back interrogatively at him, and it seemed a whole silent dialogue of: *'I don't know what's up with you, Furballs, but something's definitely **not** right, and I'm even questioning your sanity ...'* and on and on, was emanating from her steely gaze in – for him at least – a seemingly endless moment of painful awkwardness.

He squeezed his eyes tightly shut, drew in a deep breath, then opened them again, hoping the **long stare** had gone away.

It had.

"Don't worry, it won't hurt ..." said a smiling Lotty, adding, with a cheeky giggle and a wink, "... much."

A rather loud but involuntary gulp radiated out from within the vicinity of a trembling Furballs, as he nodded with weak agreement.

Oh, man! This ain't happening ...

CHAPTER 12 – TO BOLDLY GO WHERE NO STRAY HAS GONE BEFORE ...

Fatface stared out of the little triangular window as his Command Module, CATSULE 1, smoothly auto-docked with the I-STINC space station.

In the preceding hour or so he'd put on his E.V.A spacesuit and his Head Potty, (as he referred to his Space Helmet), while breathing pure oxygen for, well, he wasn't quite sure *how* long, but he knew that 'oxygen' had some important meaning that had something to do with staying alive in Outer Space and almost everywhere else in fact, even though no one – not even Furballs – had ever bothered to mention this to him.

Neither was he sure as to what was so *special* about this *oxygen stuff* that wasn't already available in good old-fashioned *air*. He certainly felt no different breathing inside the spacecraft than he had breathing the air at The Shelter, and so he had dismissed the matter, instead deciding to go over the Poop Bay Door Unsticking Procedure several times, just to be sure he'd got it right. It said:

1. Apply Oil-Can contents to Poop Bay Door.
2. Press Poop Bay Door Button.

Being a true professional, he'd tested himself by turning over the sheet of paper and speaking the instructions out loud from memory. He found that this was not so easy, and several times had got them round the wrong way. However, eventually, he satisfied himself that he could only be wrong half of the time, (as there were only two instructions), and *that* meant he'd be right at *least* the other half. And so, he decided he'd have as good a chance as any at not getting it completely wrong, (well, half of the time, anyways).

All that was left to do now was to wait until Ground Control had given him the 'GO!' for his E.V.A, and then … well … open CATSULE 1's door, (the one with the 'do not open the door' note), and make the short float over to I-STINC's jammed Poop Bay Door, where he would then apply the oil, press the Poop Bay Door Button, and release its contents into the depths of Outer Space, (along with some of that *oxygen* stuff, he assumed*),* thereby completing OPERATION SPACE DUMP.

The only other option, given any *unforeseen* happenings with his spacesuit that would mean he couldn't go outside the spacecraft, would be to open the INTERNAL DOCKING DOOR, which was currently connected directly to I-STINC's EMERGENCY POOP RELEASE PORTAL. However, this would eject the entire contents of I-STINC directly into CATSULE 1, making things ... well ... rather *unpleasant* for the attendant Catstronaut – in this case, Fatface. This was something even *he* realised would NOT be a good plan.

A familiar voice burst into his Snoopy Poopy Cap.

"Ground Control to CATSULE 1!" came the Catcom's cheery greeting. "Hey! Commander Fatface!"

"Er ... CATSULE 1 to ... er ... Ground Control!" replied Fatface, hoping he'd got it right.

"Good to hear your voice! Glad you're still with us Commander!" said the Catcom, with a nervous laugh.

"Er ... *thanks* ... I think," replied Fatface, suddenly feeling a little unsettled.

"We see you're now docked with I-STINC!"

Some snorts and giggles could be heard in the background at Mission Control. Undaunted, the Catcom continued:

"We have some words for you regarding your upcoming E.V.A."

"Yeah, I thought you might," said Fatface, flatly.

There followed a long *hiss,* during which he assumed that some complicated technical matter was being discussed on the ground, and that some further instructions would be issued, which he felt a bit nervous about because he'd only just learned *half* of the ones he'd already been given.

At last, the hissy silence was interrupted by a short message:

"Good luck!"

Fatface went to open his mouth to thank them. However, the Snoopy Poopy Cap simply made a strange 'beep' and then went completely silent.

"Hello?" he said, as a green light flashed on the NASSA standard-issue wrist computer, or 'Wristcom', that was attached to his front paw.

"OXYGEN level at 100 percent," showed the little computer screen display in luminous letters. *"E.V.A is GO! (Please now evacuate the spacecraft)."*

He recalled that his training had included a brief lecture on *'The Pristine Landscape Known as Outer Space'*. Something had been vaguely mentioned about not unzipping your spacesuit. So, knowing his manners, Fatface thought it only right that, as he approached the door with the note on, he allow a gentle tail-puff to escape in his spacesuit so as not to take it outside with him and pollute this pristine environment.

The green wrist-light suddenly changed to a flashing, urgent red, and an annoying *buzz* blasted through his ears, on and off in his Head Potty like an alarmed wasp.

FATFACE & FURBALLS' VERY BAD FURDAY

OXYGEN LEVEL at 75 to 85 percent and dropping! Toxic gaseous contaminant detected! Please purge spacesuit before exiting spacecraft!

Oh! Furballs! spluttered Fatface, inwardly, in a bit of a panic. *What do I DO?!*

He knew that his spacesuit, with its array of state-of-the-art lights, switches, tubes and multi-coloured buttons, had a 'PURGE' control somewhere and that, (if he remembered rightly), it would be 'red' when a purge was needed, and would return to a neutral 'green' once the offending gas had been expelled.

The sound of a mechanical computer voice interrupted his panic:

"Listing chemical composition of anomalous gas ..." it said, impassively.

Oh, please don't! grimaced Fatface.

Ignoring his plea, the robotic computer voice began a somewhat detailed and lengthy list:

"Nitrogen: five percent ...

Hydrogen: fifteen percent ...

Carbon Dioxide: ten percent ...

Oxygen: ten percent …

Methane: sixty percent.”

Although Fatface felt he'd heard enough, the droning computer voice continued:

“Warning: large quantity of methane detected. Some hydrogen and oxygen also present. Highly combustible. Do not expose to naked flame!”

Uncertain as to why there seemed to be such a large quantity of this methane *and* hydrogen, Fatface decided it was probably best to try and get rid of as much of both of them as possible, whilst not throwing away too much oxygen, which he apparently needed. Seeing the flashing red PURGE button just below his tummy, without hesitation, he pressed it, hoping – if nothing else – it would at least stop the incessant wasp in his ears.

It didn't.

Instead, a sort of gentle, suction *ppffffoooosshh* sound proceeded to emanate from somewhere out of the back of his spacesuit, accompanied by the computer voice (and wasp) inside his Head Potty.

"Time to (buzz) completion of (buzz) noxious gas (buzz buzz) purge," it said, metallically, in between frantic buzzing. "Estimating ... (buzz) estimating ... (buzz) ... two hundred and twenty-nine minutes ... (buzz) ... and thirty-two seconds ... (buzz)."

*That can't be right! It was only a **little** tail-puff!* thought Fatface, feeling somewhat hurt.

"Ooops! (Buzz). Incorrect assessment! (Buzz) ..." sputtered the computer:

"Recalculating ... (buzz) ... recalculating ...(buzz) ... revised estimate ... (buzz) forty-two seconds to (buzz) completion of noxious gas purge (buzz-buzz-buzz!) ..."

That's more like it! thought Fatface, somewhat relieved and hoping the 'wasp' would soon stop buzzing whilst beginning to feel more than a little irritated with the constant referral to his well-intentioned and innocent *tail-puff* as 'noxious gas'.

Predictably, his relief was short-lived, and just as he floated over to the door, (the one with the note pinned to it), another alarm began to blast – this time from inside the main cabin – synchronizing with several simultaneous, red flashing alarm lights. A second mechanical voice from CATSULE 1's Main Computer burst into action and began to chime throughout the spacecraft, filling it with dire warnings and blaring sirens.

Of course, outside the spacecraft in the cold, eerie, silent vacuum of Space, no sound can be heard, and anyone who happened to be passing by would merely have caught silent glimpses of flashing multi-coloured lights, and would have quite logically assumed that the occupant was enjoying a wild (albeit silent) disco.

However, back inside CATSULE 1, it was anything *but*.

"MAIN COMPUTER REPORT AS FOLLOWS," blasted the mechanical voice unemotionally and at full volume, (just to make sure any occupants didn't miss it):

"NOXIOUS GASES DETECTED IN MAIN CABIN. RECOMMEND FULL CAPSULE PURGE. PLEASE PUT SPACESUIT AND HELMET ON ..."

There followed a brief pause, as if it were calculating something.

"... DETECTING FOUL GASES, LISTING AS FOLLOWS ..."

*Oh, no! Not **again!*** sighed Fatface, feeling increasingly resistant to the preciseness (and very public proclamation) of information regarding his bodily emissions.

However, just as he gritted his teeth in preparation for the 'gas list', the computer interrupted itself with an urgent message:

"... AUTOMATIC DEPRESSURISATION IN SEVEN SECONDS ..."

"Oh, bendy bananas! HELP!" moaned Fatface, out loud to whomever may or may not be listening whilst amidst the din he bounced helplessly from one side of the capsule to the other, (and back again, and so on ...).

Seven seconds?! That doesn't sound very long! he thought, in a bit of a panic whilst gently patting the outside of his Head Potty, *just* to make really sure it was still sealed and securely attached to his head.

"... CORRECTION! MISCALCULATION OF AUTO-DECOMPRESS TIME-FRAME ..." sputtered the Main Computer.

"... RECALCULATING ..."

Fatface breathed a momentary sigh of relief.

Phew! That's good. I thought it seemed a bit short ...

"... REVISED CALCULATION AS FOLLOWS ... AUTO-DECOMPRESS IN ... PLEASE WAIT ... REFINING PARAMETERS ..."

Oooh! I wonder if I've got time to ...

"... **THREE** SECONDS ..."

"WHAT?!! Three seconds?!" gasped Fatface.

Oh, HELP!

A strained, descending 'whirring' sound suddenly filled the capsule, and in an instant all buzzing, alarms and sirens ceased.

"Hello?" said Fatface, peeping out from inside his Head Potty with cautious sideways glances.

He checked his Wristcom.

Spacesuit Oxygen Level = 98 percent. Purge complete. Small residue of offending gases

remains nominal but non-life-threatening. Capsule depressurization imminent. You may then evacuate spacecraft, (and remember, don't close the door, otherwise you won't get back in).

Feeling his heart begin to pound behind his ribcage, Fatface very carefully peeled away his 'DOeN'T OPpEN ThE DOR!' note, revealing the official NASSA notice beneath, which had also been scrawled on a piece of paper:

'PUT YOUR SPACESUIT AND HELMET ON BEFORE OPENING THE DOOR!'

Certain he'd done all that, and, making sure he'd got his Head Potty on securely, he peeled *that* note away to reveal the actual wording that had been (hand) painted on the door itself:

NEXT STOP: INFINITY.

And underneath *that*, in small print, it said:

Mind your step, it's very *big* out there.

And in even *smaller* print, it said:

(FYI: the proper name for 'space door' is: HATCH).

*Well, even a **door** gets a proper name!* lamented Fatface, as he began to turn the handle.

216

"Capsule depressurisation complete," came the computer voice directly into his earpiece. "If you haven't already put your Space Helmet on," it added, "well, I guess you probably won't hear this message anyhows."

"Thanks, er ... I think ..." said Fatface, uncertainly.

He turned to take one last look around inside the capsule, and made himself a promise as he surveyed the array of floating empty food packets, drink cartons and straws.

Oh, boy! I gotta tidy up when I get back!

Checking he'd got the oil-can at the ready, a last-minute thought came to grab the slab of butter, just in case he got a bit hungry while he was outdoors, (which often happened at The Shelter during the forced hour-long excursion to The Yard for his 'daily'), despite the fact that something within him was giving him a faint feeling that perhaps it might *not* be such a good idea to remove his Head Potty outside the capsule.

There had been something in his training about this, but he didn't think it was that important, otherwise his instructor would have probably mentioned it more than once.

As he turned to face the door, there came a final 'click', followed by a sort of *rushing air* sound, and then nothing except the calm rhythm of his breathing in his Head Potty as he gently pushed open the door-hatch-thingy ... (or whatever it's called).

CHAPTER 13 – THE NATIONAL LITTERY CONTEST – GRAND FINALE! ... (AT LAST)

This year's National Littery Grand Prize was a return trip in the latest, state-of-the-art orbital Tailstar Rocketplane, which, although launches like a rocket, not only returns to Earth and lands like a plane, but is designed specifically for felines to pilot and land.

Climbing to a maximum altitude of 399.9 km, the cylindrical rocket then orbits the planet below a few times or so before transforming into an aeroplane by unfurling sleek, hidden wings which open serenely just before re-entry, allowing the craft to almost nose-dive back through the atmosphere and glide to a graceful landing, whereupon the wings retract and the plane once again becomes a rocket, ready for refuelling and relaunch.

With the very latest in technological advances at his/her fingertips, (or more precisely, pawtips), the contest winner will be given a special 'Auto Pilot' trip to Space, (and back), using the latest onboard autopiloting robotics and computers.

A *Gold-Fur Standard Service* of deluxe cat food and treats plus private, curtained *Tray* area with gold-pelleted kitty litter and window for '*on-tray*' viewing of the planet beneath, as well as various comforts and luxuries, such as copious supplies of catnip, baubles and toy mice to swipe at, (and even *music* to miaow along to), awaits the winning contestant.

In other words, the winner can just sit back, relax and watch the world go by, (literally beneath them), and then be home in time for fish-nibbles.

Backstage, Furballs sat under an array of bright lights and a host of puffing, preening and pawing lady cats issuing orders to one another and arguing about this and that, lifting one of his ears up here or a paw there whilst Furballs simply closed his eyes to it all, doing his best not to run out of the place screaming.

Amidst the kittycat chatter and bright lights, he became aware of a particularly soft paw being placed under his chin and gently lifting it up.

He opened his eyelids, and there, staring serenely back, hovered Lotty. For a moment, Furballs thought she'd come to her senses and was looking deep into his eyes for some shared connecting of hearts. He then realised she was merely checking something, as her gaze switched from eye to eye, then back again.

"The left one's a bit wonky!" she shouted, coarsely, back over her shoulder to some distant part of the room.

"Oh, ok! Be right over!" came a reply from somewhere equally remote.

"Where *are* we, anyhows?" said Furballs. "I've been sittin' here for what seems like eternity!"

"Sshhh!" came Lotty's acerbic response.

"Do yooz always got to 'sshhh' me?" he replied, snappishly, trying not to move beneath … well, whatever he was being adorned with.

"Keep still!" she urged. "I can't concentrate if you keep wriggling about!"

"Here, Lotty. I've got the pins you wanted," said a little Havana Brown, as she approached and handed Lotty the pin cushion.

"Thanks, Tara," replied Lotty, as she proceeded to attach something somewhere above Furball's eyebrows, keeping the next pin poised delicately between her teeth.

"Per ... per ... p p p ... pins?" queried Furballs, a sudden wibbly wobbly sensation welling up within, causing him to blink furiously at the wavering implement that was poking out from between Lotty's clenched teeth.

"Oh, don't be a baby!" she scolded, removing the awaiting pin and fixing it somewhere behind Furballs' head. "And can you *PLEASE* stop BLINKING! What *IS* it with you?!!"

"Sorry ..." offered Furballs, uncertain as to where his usual sharpness of wit had vanished.

"Hold STILL!"

I'm trying! ... I'm trying! he thought to himself. *Boy! She's INCREDIBLE when she's angry!*

"Ok, I think we're done!" announced Lotty, finally. "Bring the mirror over!" she shouted, triumphantly.

A whole host of lady cats gathered behind Furballs in a large semi-circle whilst Lotty sidled deftly behind him and delicately covered his eyes with her paws.

"Are you ready?" she whispered excitedly down at his ear, which sounded to him, (her paws had inadvertently covered his ears too), as a somewhat muffled, *'rarr ooo eddy?'*

"What was that you just said?" he replied, feeling more than a little vexed.

Yet, before anyone had time to say, "Ta da!", Lotty uttered an eager, "Here goes!" and lifted her paws instantly away.

In unison, the entire clan of felines leaned in, fluttering their extra-long (no doubt false) eyelashes, and staring expectantly into the opposing mirror.

As Furballs opened his eyes, an involuntary "where'd I go?" escaped his lips as he sat, gaping blankly back at the image that was staring equally blankly back at him.

FATFACE & FURBALLS' VERY BAD FURDAY

Those floppy pooch ears that weren't really his anyhow had somehow been 'triangulated' into two rather oversized, pointy 'cat ears' on top of his head. Three pipe cleaners had been positioned horizontally just under his nose and fanned out to look like whiskers. His eyes had been disguised with hand-drawn cat-eyes and stuck over his own eyes, with slits so that he could (just about) still see.

A scarf arrangement had been wrapped around his neck, though he was uncertain as to why this had *anything* to do with being a cat. And, finally, a fluffy fur tail, made out of what seemed to be odd bits of whatever fur, (and anything resembling fur that could be found lying around SCRUFFS ACADEMY), had been pinned (delicately!) over the top of his own tail, with various tufts of fresh feline fluff, (whose – he didn't want to know), stuck wildly to his feet, making them look like those of a frost-hardy snowcat.

For a brief moment, he hoped that maybe it *wasn't* him staring back in the mirror. Yet, as he went to move his left paw, the imposter opposite moved *his* right paw at exactly the same instant, and when Furballs turned his head slightly to his right, the imposter turned *his* slightly to his left with an equally suspicious expression upon his face.

"Well?" said a slightly impatient Lotty. "What do you *think?*"

Furballs drew in a long, measured breath through his nose, (which was about the only thing left untampered with, and which he was still able to use with reasonable functionality). He nodded at himself a few times, ponderingly, lost in some distant, internal agreement which made everyone feel at least *somewhat* optimistic that their efforts had not been in vain.

"You see?" giggled Lotty, unable to conceal her delight at her team's work of art. "I always knew that *somewhere* beneath that canine exterior lies a *real* bona fide feline!"

Furballs didn't even bother to acknowledge the irony within himself, but just sat, staring morosely at the *monster in the mirror.*

Lotty, on the other hand, was flitting about here, there, and everywhere.

"Wait 'til you see your litter tray!" she exclaimed, exuberantly.

Oh, that's just great! thought Furballs, suddenly feeling world-weary, and shutting his eyes to all around him.

I can't wait.

*

Whilst felines of all shapes, colours and size flurried around him, preparing his 'Show Tray', Furballs sat motionlessly before the mirror with its strange reflection of the lady cats' heartfelt attempt to help him help his catstronaut friend, (currently orbiting the planet some four hundred kilometres up), in getting back to Earth in one piece.

Up until now, Furballs' life had been filled with thoughts of survival, "gettin' through each day," sarcasm, being more intelligent than Fatface, insulting Fatface, being unkind to him: in fact being *cleverer* in every way than Fatface, and generally pouring out as many insults in his direction as he could.

Yet, as he sat here now, with seemingly no other option than to go through with this *"stoopid contest,"* something began to dawn upon him.

It was no accident that he'd bumped into Fatface on that fateful day two years previously in some derelict back-street. Despite the fact that he had been "strutting along the street like the Lion King," (as Fatface had put it), deep inside, he was just a terrified little kitten, having been abandoned by his mother, who already had nine other little kitties to feed and couldn't manage another one.

Being the eldest and sole survivor of his mother's previous litter, he had felt an inward sense that it was up to him to be the one to go out into the world and fend for himself. And, seeing how much smaller and weaker his little siblings had been and how much more they needed their mother, a great weight had fallen upon his furry little shoulders.

FATFACE & FURBALLS' VERY BAD FURDAY

Having never known his father, he remembered the day when, with heavy heart, he had turned to face his mother one last time, (just in case she might beckon him back), before heading out onto the open road, alone.

He didn't have any sort of name at that point, and so, when the little puppy pooch – later hurriedly named Fatface by the Animal Catcher – came scampering towards him, Furballs couldn't believe that someone in this world actually wanted to *be* with him. Of course, Fatface then opened his mouth, and from that day on ensued the endless rounds of insults and misery.

Staring at the mirror, Furballs realised that all the nastiness he'd hurled at Fatface had really been just a thin disguise. For, deep within, that frightened little kitty was still there, waiting for someone to beckon him back to a safe, familiar world. And, sitting here now at the mercy of a hundred felines, unable to reveal his true identity and with no way of escaping whatever lay afoot within the next few hours of this *"stoopid contest,"* the full force of a lifetime of abandonment thundered through him, punishingly.

From across the way, Lotty noticed Furballs looking very forlorn. Gliding over to where he sat, and with a tilt of her head, she spoke softly into one of the ears she'd pinned onto his head.

"Hey, Furballs, where've you gone? You look like you're miles away!"

"No one's ever liked me," he moaned, without acknowledging Lotty as he stared blankly ahead at his doppelganger. "I mean, I know my mum had a hard life, and she couldn't take care of me ... yeah, I *get* that. And I'm not angry at *her*. But, I can't think of a *single* animal who's ever actually *liked* me! ..."

Lotty sat down beside him, sensing that he hadn't finished.

He hadn't.

"... I mean, there's Burt and Pertwee, I guess ..." he rambled, uncertainly.

"And Commander Fatface?" offered Lotty.

"... Yeah, Fatface, my old jail buddy."

His shoulders slumped, and he hung his head low as he continued to ruminate, miserably.

"I can't recall saying ONE nice thing to him – ever! And, yet, he's always been there! Even when I *really* didn't want him to be there ... you know ... like whenever he ate spicy chilli beans ..."

They both stared at the mirror, and sighed in perfect unison.

"... But even before I met him," he continued, "I don't know that I ever felt that anyone really *liked* me ..."

His words began to gather momentum.

"... *'Hey Furballs, how 'r yooz doin' today?'* No one's ever even bothered to ask me that! You know – *me!* Furballs the ..."

He stopped himself, just as he was about to say 'cat'.

"... Well, *I* don't even like me!" he wailed. "Soze then, how's anyone *else* supposed to?"

Lotty placed a delicate paw upon his snowcat foot.

"Furballs, what happened to you is not your fault!" she said, gently. "Just because you never had anyone *like* you when you were little, it doesn't mean you're **un-likeable** now!"

Her words stopped him in his tracks, as if a dark window in his mind had been suddenly shattered, letting in a bright blue sky and a flood of sunlight. But before he could reply, Lotty had grabbed his front paws.

"Come on!" she said, excitedly. "Your Tray's waiting!"

Dragging him up off the floor, she frog-marched him over to the backstage side-entrance, just behind the main curtain.

"Oh, and by the way," she whispered, discreetly into his ear, (which thankfully *this* time she hadn't covered up with her paws), "*I* like you!"

*No doubt about what she said **this** time*, thought Furballs, feeling like his old self again as he turned to face her and through his furry pipe cleaners, wryly sputtered:

"I know ..."

*

A special earpiece had been fitted, with a direct link to Lotty, who was now back in the dressing room.

"Testing! Testing!" came the soft, feline voice into Furballs' hidden headset as he stood behind the stage curtain, peeping through it and grimacing at the vast arena on the other side with its attendant audience, which had fallen silent with expectation of the last-minute entry.

"OW!! HEY!! Turn it *down* a bit if yooz don't mind!" he snapped back, with an edgy whisper.

"Oops! Sorry, Furballs. Is *that* better?" said Lotty, into the earpiece, with a cheeky giggle.

"Yeah, thanks … I think," he replied, wiggling a toe somewhere near to where his right ear used to be.

"Careful with those ears!" warned Lotty. "Remember, they're just pinned in place with spare bits of fluff, and if even just *one* of those pins comes out, the whole ear will flop down!"

"Yeah, I'm *aware* of the pins!" replied Furballs, grudgingly.

"Now remember," continued Lotty, "the Competition Host will ask you some questions. I've got Florence on the door listening to him through the loudspeakers. She will then relay the question to me, and I'll give you the answer. Capiche?"

Unfortunately, Furballs' recent 'capiche' conversation with Fatface in the 'Squashy Plasma Ball-ee Thingy' came hauntingly back with Lotty's words.

"Yeah … I *capiche,*" he said, sorely.

"Ok! Well, your Tray's all ready now, and all you've got to do is wait for the curtain call!"

"Capiche," said Furballs, bleakly.

From the arena, a voice could be heard booming out from the loudspeakers.

"Your Competition Host here! I've just received word of a last-minute entry!"

Someone handed him a card.

"Our final entry for tonight goes by the name of …"

He held the card, first at arm's length, then up close to his face as if to be *absolutely* certain he'd read it correctly.

"... FUR ... *BALLS?*" he said, his voice trailing upward with the last syllable.

Furballs groaned backstage upon hearing his name echo thunderously around the packed arena.

"Ok, Furballs," whispered Lotty, authoritatively, "get yourself out there!"

"Oh, yeah, thanks for the gentle encouragement!" he replied, feeling a renewed blast of his old self. "Dooz I really gotta go?" he bemoaned, into the little microphone that was hidden somewhere in his scarf. (Now he knew the reason for the scarf).

"Just GO!" blasted Lotty, with a degree of exasperation.

"Ok! Ok! I'm goin'!" snapped Furballs, with an equal gust of agitation.

Through his cardboard slits, he half-heartedly peered around the curtain, pushed it aside, and stepped out into the bright lights. What appeared to be several large Picture Box cameras and spotlights instantly swung around and aimed themselves at him, causing him to momentarily hold his paw up to his face.

Not a pin-drop could be heard as he tentatively made his way – albeit with a delicate and somewhat *pinched* walk – along the blue velvet carpet-strip, which led first to the Competition Host's desk then out into the main arena where a thousand elegantly adorned litter trays sat in regal silence. A million eager eyes burned into him as he glanced furtively from side to side.

"Please give a warm welcome," declared the Host, as Furballs approached the desk, "to our very first contestant in the 'Neutered Male' category!"

The very words Furballs had dreaded *ever* hearing, now reverberated around the arena and clanged like Notre Dame in his head.

Oh, that's just great! he thought, glumly. *I'm finally a pioneer of something – being a 'Neutered Male'!*

All at once, the loudspeakers erupted with a Flip-Flop version of 'These Paws Are Made for Scratchin' by *Catty Kintata*, and the entire audience burst into raucous cheer as everyone clapped along.

Oh, man!

Just then, a voice erupted in his head.

"Furballs! *Do* something!"

It was Lotty.

"WHAT exactly am I supposed to *DO?*" whispered Furballs from behind his pipe cleaners whilst bending his head down rather oddly at a portion of his scarf.

"You know … like *dance* or something. You have to *entertain* the audience!"

"Furballs does NOT dance!" he replied, with an edgy, irritated whisper, just as a young female kitten jumped unexpectedly out from the crowd and grabbed his front paws, swinging him around gleefully.

At that moment, Furballs noticed the Security Man, (the one who'd earlier referred to himself rather oddly as *Elsa the Lioness,* and who'd unceremoniously hurled Furballs out the back door), approaching from a dim corner, and his heart began to pound furiously.

*Oh, no! Not again! Not **HIM!***

"Come on, young lady! Leave the contestant alone!" said the man, as he lifted the young feline up by the scruff.

"I'm so sorry!" she yelped, as she dangled mid-air. "I just think you're WONDERFUL Furballs!"

A faint, plaintive cry of "I LOVE you Furballs!" could be heard echoing around the entrance corridor, followed by the familiar sound of *that* door being slammed.

*What was all **that** about?* thought Furballs, as he turned back to face the Host, relieved – if somewhat bemused – that he hadn't been recognised.

"Oh, my apologies!" said the Host, somewhat flustered. "We accept NO harassment of our contestants, even if it's one of your most ardent fans you've brought along with you!"

"I've never seen her before in my life!" countered Furballs, defensively, feeling somewhat bamboozled.

"Oh ... erm ... well!" replied the Host, with some embarrassment.

Furballs nodded in the direction of the Security Man.

"I'm just relieved *that* guy didn't recog ..."

"SSSHHHH!!!" came a loud, scratchy voice into his earpiece.

"OUCH!" blurted Furballs, thrusting a paw protectively up to his right ear.

"Are you OK?" said the Host. "I know these fans can be a bit of a nuisance," he offered, meekly.

"Yeah! I'm good!" replied Furballs, irritably. "Can we just get on with this thing?"

"Oh, yes, of course!" said the Host.

"Calm DOWN!" came a soothing voice into his ear.

"I can't *calm down* ..." whispered Furballs, defensively into his scarf, "... if yooz keep turning UP the volume!"

"I'm sorry, Furballs," said Lotty. "I was just chatting with Tara, and must have pressed the wrong button!"

"Yeah, well, *you* try being out here with half the world's population of felines and *most* of the world's supply of kitty litter!" insisted Furballs. "It *stinks* out here!"

"Ssshh!" rebuffed Lotty. "And stop talking to your scarf! You're starting to look suspicious!"

"In case you hadn't noticed," he countered, with increasing annoyance, "I'm a dog dressed up as a crazy cat with cardboard eyes, whiskers any self-respecting animal would not be seen *dead* in, the weirdest looking feet that even *Big Foot* would be embarrassed by, and ..."

He sucked in a humungous gulp of air, just to make sure his point would be heard.

"... On top of all that I'm wearing a scarf! I mean, what self-respecting animal ... never mind feline ... wears a *scarf?* So, yeah, you could say I look just a teensy-weensy bit suspicious!"

*And, boy, that doesn't include that whole **other** part of this story!* he thought, silently, while shaking his head in agreement with himself.

"Ok, Furballs, you've made your point!" replied Lotty, ignoring his ranting insults about her all-girl team's costume design. "Now stop talking and listen to me!" she asserted. "The Host is going to ask you some questions. Wait for my answers. I repeat – do NOT say anything until you've heard from me! Capiche?"

"Yeah, I *capiche* alright!" he grumbled, with a huff. "And can we stop saying 'capiche'?"

"Sshhh! I told you – DON'T talk to the scarf!"

Furballs went to say 'OK' but instead became aware of a strange, uncomfortable, *hot* sort of sensation creeping up the back of his neck. Delicately crooking his head around, (so as not to disturb any of those pins), he noticed that the Host was staring down at him with an intense, expectant gaze.

"Are you ok, sir?" said the man, courteously.

Sir? thought Furballs. *Me? A* **Sir?**

"Oh, sure!" he replied, casually. "Just checking my ... er ... scarf."

"May we then, well ... *proceed* with the competition?" said the Host, raising an eyebrow.

Furballs nodded, obediently, as the man picked up his microphone.

"Welcome, er ... Fur ... *Balls!* ..." he announced, to a round of applause.

Feeling a slight *tug* upon his jacket, the Host looked down.

"It's *Furballs* ... yooz know ... all one word!" said Furballs. "Not *'Fur'*, and then wait half a millennium to say, *'balls'*. No! Just ... *Furballs*. Capiche?"

"Oh!" said the Host, feeling rather ashamed. "I *do* apologise, sir ... I mean ... *Furballs.*"

"That's more like it. Sorry to interpurrupt," said Furballs, with a *swoosh* of a paw to encourage the man to continue.

"Yes! Well then! Where was I? Oh, yes! We will first take a look at your Tray, and then ask you some questions, after which there is one final test: to correctly sing the words of a well-known song ..."

Er ... did he just say 'sing'? thought Furballs, a sudden swimmy sensation filling his head as he tuned out the Host's remaining words.

Oh, man ...

"Lotty!" he whispered, with a desperate rasp.

However, given his most recent, rash comments to her regarding his catsuit costume, he realised he'd probably overstepped the mark slightly.

His earpiece remained silent.

"Let's go over to your Tray first!" said the Competition Host.

"LOTTY!" whispered Furballs, becoming increasingly frantic.

Still nothing.

"OK! OK! I'm SORRY, Lotty! I didn't mean what I said about your catsuit!"

"Don't panic, Furballs, I've got your back – literally!" came Lotty's soft, familiar voice. "You're forgiven. Now stop talking and just listen! Go over to your Tray, and when the Host asks you questions about it, wait for my answer! Capiche?"

"Yeah, yeah ... anything! I'm desperate, Lotty! I can't sing for catnip, let alone this ..."

He stopped himself before the word 'stoopid' could escape.

"... contest. So yeah, I *capiche.*"

"Great! Now, stop talking and get your hindquarters over to your Tray!"

Inspecting the Trays was a white-coated feline figure which, from behind at least, Furballs thought he recognised but which simultaneously gave him the collywobbles.

Bending over, buried deep in its inspection of his Tray, the figure sniffed and prodded and studied the array of flowers, pom poms and glittered kitty litter that adorned it. Some contemplative miaows of curiosity and approval could occasionally be heard as Furballs neared.

It was then that he noticed the centrepiece of Lotty's lady cats' pellety creation. A miniature feline figurine of Commander Fatface, proudly holding his Head Potty, (tucked under one of his front legs whilst dangling a pooperlooper bag from his other outstretched paw), adorned the middle area of the Tray, with litter pellets of all colours streaking outwards like rainbow rays from the Sun.

The words: 'OPerRAshiOn SpAsSe DuUmP' had been piped in a circle around the little figurine.

Sheesh! I thought Fatface was the only one who couldn't spell! noted Furballs, somewhat stupefied.

But it was the little feline decoration that struck at his core. For, unknown to the outside world, stood a miniature doppelganger of the *real* Furballs. And back behind the cardboard slits of the bigger Furballs, a few drops of salty liquid leaked out from his big, borrowed puppy eyes.

However, his trance was soon interrupted by a disconcertingly familiar voice.

"Good evening, Fur ... *Balls,*" it said, in a wizened, slightly shrill tone from behind its white coat.

"It's ... *Furballs* ... not ... *Fur* ... blank space ... *balls.* All-one-word ... *Furballs,*" he said, with a sort of flat, unapologetic impatience.

He was just about to add "capiche?" when, having completed her inspection, the white-coated figure stood up and turned to face him.

A ghostly chill streaked down his spine.

It was the Burmese Registrar who so very kindly had had him violently expelled earlier that day.

Oh, dangling deer-droppings! groaned Furballs. *I may as well just go home now ... well, if I **had** one,* he pondered, dejectedly.

"I *do* apologise, Sir!" she said, holding out a truce-seeking paw.

"Er ... sure!" replied Furballs, as he returned the gesture and shook hers with his front snowcat foot.

What's with all the 'Sir' business? he thought, none the wiser.

"There's something *familiar* about you," she said, with a sliding whine. "Yet ... I can't ... quite ... place it," she added, as she circled him, inspectingly.

Good! he thought, brazenly, as his heart began to thump.

"Oh, well! It's no matter," she concluded. "I apologise for the mispronunciation of your name."

"Oh ... that's ... er ..."

Unusually, Furballs found himself lost for words.

"... *cool,*" he said at length, albeit somewhat shakily.

The Burmese smiled, and with a slithery turn of her head, declared:

"Well, I have to say, *Furballs,* I have *never* in all my years as Registrar and Judge of this competition seen a Tray as beautifully and uniquely adorned as yours! Congratulations! You've won the 'Best Litter Tray' category!"

"Er … oh! Thanks! Yeah! … great!" said Furballs, suddenly feeling an instinctive urge to escape.

"No, really!" said the Burmese. "It's a work of art!"

To the sound of Catty Kintata's hit song, the entire audience erupted in applause and began to sing:

"… These paws are made for scratchin'

And that's just what they'll do!

One of these days these paws are gonna

Scratch all over YOU!"

Everyone cheered, as the Competition Host then led Furballs away from the 'Tray' section and over towards a podium.

"Did you hear that Lotty?" he whispered, furtively, *en route* to the awaiting panel of questioners. "They love what you girls did to my Tray!"

He became silent for a moment.

"And, well, I kinda do too," he added, humbly.

"Yes, Furballs," replied Lotty, "we're all listening to you here! The girls are huddled behind the main curtain. We wouldn't miss this for anything!"

"Any progress on the song?" he queried, hesitantly.

"It's all sorted!" said Lotty, reassuringly. "Now go do your thing!"

"That's what I'm afraid of ..." he replied, wearily.

He approached the podium, in front of which a panel of human judges silently sat, all eyes upon him as he stepped up onto the little platform.

The instant his paws touched it, it lit up with a sort of pinky-mauve light, the surrounding lights of the arena dimming to almost nothing. A bright spotlight then beamed directly down upon him, causing him to squint behind his cardboard slits.

The Competition Host made an announcement:

"And now for Round Two! Can *Furballs* ..."

He looked across at Furballs, who nodded back approvingly for pronouncing his name correctly.

"... answer each of these two questions correctly? Let's find out!"

Instantly, the music stopped, and an expectant hush fell upon the crowd.

"First question!" declared the Host.

A spotlight fell upon the first Panel-Judge, who stared squarely back at Furballs.

"Name a breed of feline with eyes that are different colours!"

Oh, help! I only knows those that came to The Shelter! I guess most of them **did** *actually have two eyes, but I never really looked that close, like, to see what colour they were!*

"Now, stay calm!" came Lotty's familiar voice. "I'm just checking ..."

Well, hurry up! thought Furballs, as he tried to convey a look of intelligent thought.

"It's ... *Khao Manee,*" said Lotty.

"K ... O ... Man ... eee," said Furballs, robotically.

"Easy does it!" said Lotty. "Try to sound a little more ... well, *natural!*"

I'm trying! he thought, as he scratched his scarf in an attempt to indicate to Lotty that he was doing his best.

"Correct!" said the Host, to a cheer from the crowd. "Next question!"

The second Panel-Judge appeared under a spotlight.

"Name a famous Egyptian feline!"

"Sounds like a trick question to me!" said Lotty. "Hold on, we're just checking ..."

Furballs tried to look as if he were pondering thoughtfully, but in doing so inadvertently scratched his scarf, pulling out his earpiece in the process. Thankfully no one seemed to notice except Furballs, who visibly began to twitch.

"Er ... Mmm ..." he mumbled, stalling for time as he began to search furtively around his scarf for the wire, flinging it *this* way and *that* in grand, sweeping gestures.

"We need your answer," said the Panel-Judge, brusquely.

"Er ... yeah ... I'm just ..."

"*What* are you *doing?*" whispered the Competition Host, nervously, as he leaned in toward Furballs, shrugging his shoulders.

"Erm ..."

A thin wire suddenly swished upwards behind a length of scarf, which Furballs deftly swirled around his neck whilst pretending to scratch his ear and grappling with the little earpiece at the wire's end.

The Host, becoming visibly perturbed, waved his hands about, impatiently.

"I have to insist that you answer the ..."

"Got it!" shouted Furballs, to the puzzlement of the Panel-Judges.

"Where have you *been?*" came Lotty's sudden, exasperated voice into the earpiece. "I've been shouting the answer to you for the past few minutes!"

"Oh!" said Furballs, out loud, seemingly to the judges but aiming it at the little microphone, wherever *that* had gone, for he knew not which bit of scarf it was now hiding in.

"I'm sorry about that!" he bawled, hoping Lotty had heard him.

The Panel-Judges exchanged several disapproving glances.

"Are you listening now?" she said, curtly, and without giving Furballs a chance to answer added, "Well, you'd *better* be!"

"Yes! I'm listening!" he shouted, to the consternation of the Host and Panel.

By now, the audience had started to get a bit restless, and an occasional heckle of "Boo!" and "Get off!" could be heard from disgruntled spectators.

"Ok, here it is!" said Lotty, hurriedly, as she proceeded to pronounce the word slowly:

"TOO-TAN-CAT-MOON. And," she suggested, *"try to say it a bit more … elegantly!"*

Furballs drew in a deep breath, seemingly sucking in the entire arena, as everyone leaned in to make sure they didn't miss anything.

"Tootancatmoon," he said, in as casual manner as he could muster whilst holding his scarf down flatly at his sides and blinking furiously, which only made him appear more tense and which provoked some questioning looks from the Panel-Judge, who merely twitched her nose before uttering one single word:

"Correct."

A gasp, followed by a sigh of relief, echoed around the arena as Furballs stood on the little podium, looking tentatively about himself.

"So, what happens n ..."

But before he could finish his question, the entire arena erupted in a thunderous cheer as the Host grabbed Furballs' front paws and congratulated him enthusiastically.

"Er ... thanks," said Furballs, feeling somewhat mystified.

The audience quickly quieted themselves with a splattering of 'shooshes', eager to get to the next round.

"You've made it through the first two rounds!" said the Host. "Now we come to our third and final round – 'Singing The Words of A Song to the Tune of Another!'"

"Ok, Furballs," came Lotty's voice, "we've got you covered. As soon as he gives you the title of the songs, we'll be ready for you! Remember, we're lady cats, and we have *beautiful* singing voices!"

Furballs couldn't recall many of the 'lady cats' at The Shelter having been in possession of particularly pleasant voices. But, oh well, he wasn't really in a position to argue at present. Besides, a new, much more worrying concern had arisen.

"Wait! I thought I just had to sing any old song I like! And now I've not only gotta sing a song, but fit the words of a completely different song *to* it? And I don't even got to *chooz*?!" he whispered, sharply and scratchily into his scarf, his grammar going completely out the window.

Feeling the spotlight turn once again upon him, he swept the scarf impatiently around his neck and stood there, twitching irritably behind his pipe cleaners, which had begun to visibly droop on one side.

A green light illuminated a different Panel-Judge, who looked suspiciously down across his spectacle rims at Furballs as he uttered the words:

"Please sing the words of the song ..."

He then shuffled some pieces of paper around before nodding agreeably at finding a suitable title.

"... 'Happy Birthday' to the tune of, 'Oh My Darling, Clementine."

"Ahem!" coughed Furballs. "Would you mind repeating that please?" he spluttered, hoping Lotty had heard it all, and trying to buy some time.

The Panel-Judge gave Furballs a somewhat disapproving glare, rattled his piece of paper abruptly, and repeated the instruction, albeit a bit more slowly and deliberately this time.

"Please ... would ... you ... sing ... the ... words ... of ... 'Happy Birthday' ... to ... the ... tune ... of ... 'Oh My Darling, Clementine'!"

"Ok, don't panic, Furballs," came Lotty's slightly panicky voice. "I'm on to it! Can you stall for a minute?"

"*How?*" he whispered, feverishly, with a sort of fake cough into his scarf. "What am I supposed to do? Tell a *joke?*"

No response came, and he assumed that the microphone must have slipped down to some remote southerly location of his catsuit.

"Oh, yeah ..." stuttered Furballs, to the Panel-Judge. "Of course! ... er ... just to make sure I've *really* got that right, you mean, the *tune* of 'Happy Birthday' to the *words* of 'Oh My Darling, Clementine'?"

The Panel-Judged huffed whilst giving visibly incredulous glances in the direction of his co-judges.

"I think I spoke clearly enough!" he said, with a raised eyebrow.

"Oh, well, yes, er ..." fumbled Furballs. "... Well, you see, I have this *inner ear* problem, and sometimes it's almost as if I've got someone talking *inside* my head at the same time as someone *outside* my head ... you know, like you! It's really strange!" he said, shrugging his shoulders, nonchalantly.

"Goodness me!" exclaimed the Panel-Judge, barely containing his irritation. "Oh, very well! I'll explain it *again* then! Please sing the *WORDS* of 'Happy Birthday' to the *TUNE* of 'Oh My Darling, Clementine'!"

Lotty!

"Ok, Furballs!" came Lotty's cheery, (and somewhat relieved), voice. "My girls are on it! We're just rehearsing!"

"Rehearsing?!" he whispered, with a frantic sort of muted disbelief. "Now?" he added, incredulously. "I don't have time for ... *rehearsing!*" He emphasised the last word with a frenzied rasp.

Seeing the judges begin to look at their watches, Furballs began to cough rather hoarsely.

"I'm so ... (cough) ... sorry! (Cough, splutter, cough). I seem to have a ... (cough) ... frog in my throat!"

"Ok!" affirmed Lotty. "We're ready now!"

"About time!" whispered Furballs, under his breath.

"Oh, stop your whining!" she rebuked. "And get ready to *sing!*"

"In your own time, *please!*" said the Panel-Judge, clearing his throat with an impatient retch.

An unpleasant, scratchy noise began to filter down through Furballs' earpiece, causing him to grimace and rattle his head about somewhat disturbingly.

"Are you alright?" said the Panel-Judge.

"Er … yeah! I'm fine!" lied Furballs. "It's just that *inner ear* trouble again."

"We're just tuning our voices, Furballs," said Lotty. "Ok, here goes!" she declared. "The choir will sing one line at a time, and then you sing it out loud! Capiche?"

Uncertain as to whether the term 'choir' was appropriate for the noise entering his earpiece, Furballs nonetheless nodded, hoping 'Florence behind the curtain' would see and give the go-ahead to the choir.

She must have done so, as a delicate, finely tuned sound began to filter down the wire and into Furballs' ear, sending him into a slight swoon for an instant before it abruptly stopped.

"Ok, Furballs. Now sing what we just sang!" said Lotty.

Feeling a dreadful churning in his tummy area, Furballs drew in a deep breath, opened his mouth, (behind his pipe cleaners), and began to sing:

"HAPPY BIRTHDAY, HAPPY BIRTHDAY, HAPPY BIRTHDAY TOOOOO …. YOOOOOOOZ …"

"Here comes the next bit!" whispered Lotty.

Furballs listened while pretending to take a particularly long, deep breath.

"Go Furballs!" she said.

"HAPPY BIRTHDAY, DEAR ..." he began until a sudden panic gripped him.

Who am I supposed to sing to?

A two-syllable name popped instantly into his head. Without waiting to analyse the potential repercussions of basically telling the whole world who he had feelings for, out came the word:

"... *LOTT... EEEEE ...*"

He listened for the final line, but all that came down the wire was a gaggle of female giggles, followed by a rather coarse, teasing cackle from some distant part of the dressing room:

"... Oi! Lotty! I think he likes you!"

Lotty's chuckling voice could just about be heard above the din.

"Oh, stop it girls! Come on! Let's finish the song!"

CASS CLARK

The spotlight, whose unrelenting glare Furballs had only just got used to, suddenly narrowed its beam and intensified its brightness even more so as it focused directly onto his face, which by now had lost a couple of whiskers, and one of his cardboard eyes had slipped sideways, along with a drooping ear that had lost a pin.

Through the surrounding gloom, Furballs could just about discern the glum, shadowy, suspecting faces of the Panel-Judges, with their now-elongated shadows cast by the floodlight, giving them an especially eerie, unwelcoming presence.

The entire arena had become so silent that Furballs wondered if everyone was still there, or if they'd all just quietly crept home. So, as if it were a deliberate part of his 'act', he took a sweeping bow, flung his scarf around his head and, bending over, waited.

At last, the final melody and words filtered through into his earpiece, and as he slowly stood himself up he swept open the scarf like a giant cape and bellowed out the final words with grand, swishing here-comes-the-end-of-the-song gestures:

"HAPPY ... BIRTH ... DAY ... TO ..."

With one final, elegant pause, he drew in the deepest breath, whereupon he inadvertently stood on the lost pin, went up a full octave, and at the top of his voice blasted out the final note:

"... YOOOOOOOOOOOOOOOOOOOOOOZZZ!"

At which point the remaining pipe cleaner fell off its hinge, along with the cardboard eye, causing Furballs to hurriedly sweep his scarf across one side of his face, covering up the now decidedly poochy-looking exposed area.

All was silent as he held his position, statuesque upon the little podium, eyes darting from side to side under the intense spotlight, which suddenly softened as the entire arena began to light up.

As his eyes readjusted, Furballs saw – not an empty space as he had imagined – but every member of the audience standing by their seats, along with row upon row of cats standing by their litter trays, every single one staring back at *him*.

Even the Panel-Judges had stood up, as had the Host, and out of the corner of his eye he saw Lotty and the 'choir' appear from behind the curtain, (along with Florence).

All at once, the entire arena erupted in the loudest, most jubilant cheering and applause, as every feline and human in the building, (including the Security Man), showed their appreciation.

The Host ran wildly over to Furballs and grabbed his front paws, shaking them violently up and down.

"Congratulations, Furballs! You're this year's National Littery Contest winner!"

"I am?" he said, in a daze.

A soft, cheeky voice filtered into his ear.

"Hey! Furballs! Remember me?"

It was Lotty.

"Where are you?" he said, looking over to the dressing room area.

"Right behind you!" she said.

He swung himself around.

"Ta da!" she announced, with a bow, and handed him a flower.

"Would you take this into Space for me?" she asked, looking up at him with big, sincere eyes. "It'll make me feel a bit closer to my Mum, wherever she is now."

"Yeah, anything for you Lotty," replied Furballs, suddenly remembering he was still wearing Fatface's *pooch-suit*, and consequently drawing himself away, (despite not wanting to).

The Competition Host beckoned Furballs over to his desk.

"Go! Go! Go!" said Lotty, shooing him off.

"So, Furballs, how does it feel to be this year's winner?" asked the Host, as Furballs approached.

"Er ... well ..." he replied, not wishing to lie, but sensing it *might* not be such a good idea to confess to never having wanted to enter this *'stoopid contest'*. He suddenly felt slightly ashamed at having called it that.

"... It feels, er ... surprising!"

The audience laughed along, agreeably.

"How long have you been interested in litter tray design?" asked the Host.

Oh, man!

Furballs closed his eyes and tried not to hear what he was about to say.

"I've always *dreamed* of entering this competition! It's always been my greatest ambition! I'm so *proud* to be here!"

He hoped that would be enough.

It was ... sort of.

"One final question then, Furballs," said the Host. "Are you looking forward to going into Space?"

"Well," he pondered, remembering the reason he had entered the contest in the first place. "I'll let you know when we get back."

The Host, not noticing that Furballs had said 'we' and not 'I', rounded up the interview.

"Do you have any questions about going into Space, Furballs?" he said, thrusting the microphone up to the one remaining pipe cleaner.

"Yeah, I got a question!" he replied. "Dooz I got to take this stoopid scarf with me?"

The audience chortled with delight.

"No!" said the Host, with a hearty chuckle.

And with that, the interview ended.

To the sounds of the song, 'Pooper-Scooper' by Adda, Furballs was led out of the arena to claim his prize, and made his way to the area where he would prepare for his spaceflight aboard the Tailstar rocket plane.

Just as he was about to exit the arena, he felt someone tap his shoulder, and turned to see a bloodhound-cross mutt staring longingly at the remaining cardboard eye.

"Man, I've never seen a cat quite like you before!" said the stranger.

If only you knew! thought Furballs.

"What are you doing afterwards?" insisted the starstruck interloper.

"Er ... something else," replied Furballs before running as fast as he could into the *'Winners Only'* prize-claiming area.

CHAPTER 14 – PAL! OPEN THE POOP BAY DOOR! ... MIAOW!

With his head poking out of CATSULE 1's hatch, (or *Space Door* as he had finally decided to call it), Fatface surveyed the dark vacuum, turning a full circle until he was back where he started.

Why is it always night up here? he wondered.

He noted that although the stars weren't twinkling like they do from the Shelter Yard, their light was now so piercing and intense that he couldn't take his eyes off them.

With his oil-can safely stowed in his belt and his slab of *Emergency Butter* even more securely attached, Fatface eased his way out of the capsule, checked that his tether was attached to something solid at one end and his spacesuit at the other, and gently pushed himself away from CATSULE 1, out into the void of space and stars.

FATFACE & FURBALLS' VERY BAD FURDAY

A couple of miniature Paw Jet Propellers – or PJPs – came as standard with his Deluxe Spacesuit, and consisted of two small cannisters – one on the paw-end of each front leg – which catstronauts could use to control and adjust their spacewalks. A limited supply, it would be enough to manoeuvre in small increments or enable catstronauts to return to the safety of their spacecraft in an emergency, should they need to.

Pressing the right-hand PJP, he suddenly found himself rotating slowly in one direction. He then pressed the left-hand PJP which reversed the spin, and after a few minutes of trying one way then the other, he managed to steady himself until he floated seemingly motionlessly above planet Earth.

"Hey, Furballs!" he said, out loud inside his Head Potty. "I hope you're ok! I'm just about to go over to I-STINC and unstick the door! There is a computer over there that I have to talk to and get it to release the pooperlooper bags. I guess after I've done that, then … my job's done …"

He paused momentarily.

"... And, well ..."

His thoughts trailed off, and a strange, peaceful silence came over him. It wasn't *bad,* and it wasn't *good.* It just made him feel very calm.

He watched as the giant globe beneath him rotated serenely.

"The Shelter looks so pretty from up here," he continued. "I never knew it was so *big!* I like the blue bits best, and there's lots of that! There are some white, fluffy bits too mixed in with some green and brown bits, but I think the white fluffy bits look most pretty above the blue. I guess The Yard is bigger than I thought!

"Hey, buddy! I don't know what you're doing down there, or even where you are. But I know you're doing something important, whatever it is. Anyways, I just wanted to say, I don't know what's going to happen after I've fixed the door, but I kinda feel ok about it all. And I just wanted you to know. I guess that self-help book helped after all!"

He looked at his Space Watch.

FATFACE & FURBALLS' VERY BAD FURDAY

"Ok, I gotta go do this thing now. I hope you're ok down there, wherever you are, and that you're taking good care of my pooch-suit! I kind of miss it, but I'm slowly getting used to wearing your catsuit. It's a bit tight and skinny in places, but it works ok. Well, see you around, buddy."

He pressed both PJPs and zigzagged his way over to the awaiting I-STINC space station, which loomed like a dark, gigantic cube, rotating slowly and sinisterly, blocking out starlight from anything that dared to hide behind it.

As he got closer, an uncomfortable, wobbly feeling filled Fatface's tummy, which made him feel that he might not be able to complete his mission. It all seemed so much *bigger* than him, and the 'cube' didn't exactly look very friendly.

However, there was plenty of sunlight, and Fatface had noted how different the Sun looked in the blackness of Space, compared to when it was surrounded by blue sky.

CASS CLARK

Even the Sun looks a bit lonely from up here, he thought, as he approached the space station.

The words, 'INTERNATIONAL SEWERAGE TANK IN SPACE CONTAINER (I-STINC)', glimmered with gold letters in the sunlight on one side of the cube, and Fatface could see the little Poop Bay Door, which, when opened, would release the cube's contents of pooperlooper bags in a steady stream.

On the other side of the cube was another door – or *hatch* for those insistent on using the correct technical terms – which housed a small, isolated compartment that contained the state-of-the-art 'PROTOCOL ALIGNMENT LINEAR' computer, or 'PAL' for short.

It was Fatface's job to communicate with PAL and re-start it to resume normal operation, as it had gone into *Standby* mode following the whole door-sticking thing, and the guys back at NASSA had lost the remote-control device, (probably down the back of the sofa), so were unable to implement the re-start from the ground.

As he approached the Poop Bay Door, Fatface grabbed one of the handles that were attached to the station, and with his other gloved paw unhooked the little oil-can from his spacesuit, removing its cap.

He'd remembered from his training to then push the dispenser button on top of the can *gently,* and to apply one tiny drop of oil at a time, given that – in Space – any liquid would turn into little globules and float away, (as he had discovered with his drinks cartons).

The added problem of temperature had also been addressed by the team at NASSA, who had developed a special additive for the oil so that it would stay runny even in outer space, where the temperature drops to what Fatface seemed to recall as something known as *'minus two hundred and seventy centipedes'.*

A chap named 'Kelvin' had also been mentioned as, (apparently), he too had a very low temperature of 'absolutely nothing', but no one had ever bothered to tell Fatface whereabouts in space you were supposed to find him so that you could warm him up a bit. (Yet another possible lecture at CATBASE where Fatface may have 'drifted off').

A special keep-me-warm foil, with its futuristic technology that could keep smallish items at room temperature in Outer Space, had been wrapped around the oil-can. The trick then, (to Fatface's thinking), was to get the oil onto the Poop Bay Door as quickly as possible before all those *centipedes* arrived.

"Ok, then," he said, talking himself through the procedure, "all I have to do is press the Dispender Button, or whatever they call it."

The big red button on top of the can had the words 'PRESS GENTLY!' written in equally big letters.

"Here goes!" he said, as he hovered his space glove precariously over the button, at which moment a mechanical voice blasted into his Head Potty, saying: "Intruder alert!", causing him to jump in his fur and accidentally hit the button hard.

"Oh!" he shrieked, as the entire contents of the oil-can streamed out in a long, greasy chain of globules, floating irretrievably away into Deep Space.

"Oh dear, Fatface," he said, trying to console himself, "what are we going to do?"

He floated there motionlessly for several moments as he watched his one hope of successfully completing the mission trickle away like an oily necklace toward the distant Sun, where he assumed things might be a bit warmer, and where 'Mr Kelvin' might finally be able to warm himself up.

"Oh, what am I gonna tell Furballs?" he said, to himself. "He already thinks I'm stupid. Oh, I wish he was here! He's the clever one! He'd get me out of this!"

A strange sensation flooded his senses, almost like an imaginary soft hammer banging on his head that wouldn't leave him alone until he listened.

He remembered he'd brought his slab of butter with him, just in case he'd got hungry while unsticking the Poop Bay Door. However, given that the whole 'unsticking business' had gone a bit wrong, he reasoned that he wouldn't need to eat the butter now, and so it occurred to him that he could actually *use* it to unstick the door.

This strange sensation bloomed into a wild feeling, like a great big 'YES!' that had burst open inside him.

Carefully removing the outer wrapping, he began to scrape the slab around the entire Poop Bay Door seal, which instantly froze the butter, making it look like cake-frosting.

Unperturbed by this, Fatface remembered that part of his NASSA Standard Issue Equipment, (or 'stand-on-a-tissue' as he liked to call it), included a small laser pointer which produced a red beam of light. Past experience had taught him that 'red' meant 'hot', and so, applying that logic to this problem, he grabbed the little pointer, which was attached to his Utility Belt, and without disconnecting it, (for he didn't want to lose *that* as well), he aimed it at the ring of butter around the Poop Bay Door, and pressed the 'ON' button.

At first, it seemed that nothing was happening as he made a complete circle with the laser. But something inside him seemed to be urging him to keep going.

"I guess I'll try again," he said, with a shrug.

However, after several circuits, he stopped.

"Maybe if I just aim at one area and leave the laser there a bit longer, it might melt it a bit more!" he pondered, audibly. "I know it doesn't make any sense, but I really have nothing left to lose … well, except the laser pointer," he reasoned, with a reluctant sigh.

"Intruder alert!"

There it was again! That strange, mechanical, slightly alarmed-sounding voice. Wherever it was coming from, it seemed to know that Fatface was trying to 'get in'.

It must be the PAL computer, he pondered, dreamily, as his thoughts drifted off while he absent-mindedly held the laser at the same splodge of butter.

Unexpectedly, the Poop Bay Door moved slightly, as if it were dislodging itself from some frozen prison.

"Poop Bay Door reconfigured!" came the computer voice.

"Is that good?" said Fatface, feeling slightly alarmed.

"Poop Bay Door unstuck. Fully operational," said the monotone voice. "Intruder alert disengaged."

"I did it!" said Fatface, wishing Furballs had been there to share the moment yet at the same time thinking that perhaps he would have sorted all this out much sooner anyway. Nonetheless, this didn't dampen Fatface's newfound confidence.

"Now all I have to do is go over to the other door, get inside and restart the computer!"

Gripping its various handles, Fatface floated his way around the vast cube of I-STINC and arrived at the other little *space door* that opened up into the home of its mechanical inhabitant, PAL.

"Identify yourself!" came the metallic reply.

"Erm ... oh, yes! Commander Fatface!" said Fatface, with a slight, introductory cough.

"Checking ... Checking ... Authorisation needed ..."

"Authorisation?" he queried.

"Please state entry code."

Fatface scratched his Head Potty.

Entry code? Now what was it again? Oh yes! I think I've got it!

He rehearsed the NASSA-issued password a couple of times, drew in a deep breath, and stated:

"PAL! Open the Poop Bay Door!"

"Password incomplete," came the instant, emotionless response.

Incomplete?

With another scratch of his Head Potty, he floated up and down outside the metal monolith, with no one to help and a whole planet below him with people that *could* help but for whatever reason had thought it prudent that he manage things all by himself.

I guess they decided I was the best one for the job, he thought in his usual manner but with a sudden flash of realisation.

Which means, I can dooz this! he said to himself excitedly, mimicking Furballs.

Ok, I'll try again!

"PAL! Open the Poop Bay Door!"

"Password incomplete."

Oh, boy!

"Well, can you give me a *clue?*" he offered.

"Please state nature of clue requested."

Oh, lingering limpets!

"Well, which bit is the bit where it's incomplete?" spluttered Fatface, getting his words in a bit of a tangle.

"After the word 'door'," said PAL.

"Oh, ok! Thanks!" said Fatface, as his brain went into a sort of *overdrive* mode and he tried to remember what his instructor had said comes after the word 'door'.

PAL! Open the Poop Bay Door .... something ... mmm ... oh ... what was it?

About thirty minutes, (and half a tank of oxygen later), Fatface felt a little bit more certain that he'd remembered at least *some* of it correctly.

Here goes!

Having realised that if he *didn't* get it right this time, he wouldn't have enough air left in his spacesuit, (you know, that *normal* stuff we breathe, not all this fancy *oxygen* business), and he'd have to return to CATSULE 1 having failed to complete OPERATION SPACE DUMP, he drew in another deep breath and hesitated momentarily.

Feeling a rather strange, uncomfortable *pressing* feeling all over himself that was very unpleasant and which he hoped would *go away*, an old canine saying popped into his head:

'No pressure, no dinner!'

Although he had never understood *exactly* what that meant, he sensed that it was something to do with doing something important when you felt like you really didn't *want* to but that something better would happen afterwards if you *did*. So, you really had no choice but to do the thing anyway.

Ok, Fatface! This is it! Here we go:

"PAL! Open the Poop Bay Door! ..."

He paused, and with his heart thumping in his chest and his spacesuit flashing, 'Oxygen Level: CRITICAL!', uttered the final word:

"... MIAOW!"

A horrible, sick, trembly feeling engulfed him, as his response was met with stony silence. Those old thoughts of 'You're a failure!', 'You're stupid!', 'You'll always be a let-down!' came hurtling back through his mind, and he felt his bottom lip begin to wobble slightly.

That's it. I've failed, he thought, dismally. *I'm sorry NASSA. I'm sorry Burt, Pertwee and Shelter Lady. I'm sorry, Furballs ...*

"Entry authorised!" came a voice. "You now have ten seconds to enter the main Computer Bay ... ten ... nine ... eight ..."

"Wer ... WHAT?!" said Fatface, the sudden shock waking him up from his desolate musings.

The little hatch-door opened slowly to reveal an array of different-coloured lights bedecking the entire Computer Bay, flickering on and off continually in their myriad conversations. Strange little mechanical noises clicked and clacked, with an occasional whir and click of something spinning and locking into place.

"... seven ... six ... five ..."

"Ok! I'm coming in!" gushed Fatface, as he squeezed himself through the little opening, which was *just* wide enough to fit his life-support pack through.

Once inside, the little door closed, and Fatface sat, staring around at all the different lights and switches.

"Computer Bay pressurised," announced PAL. "Please remove Space Helmet."

"It's a *Head Potty!*" grumbled Fatface, as he lifted his off.

"Noted," said PAL, whose point of communication was represented by a little, round lens-shaped red light that lit up whenever the computer spoke.

Fatface sensed a sort of *presence* all around him, as if PAL were indeed alive. He also sensed an oddness about it, as if PAL had been left alone for far too long and was studying this intruder into its world.

Fatface searched around for the 'Restart' switch which, (he'd been informed), was green in colour and had the words: RE-START SWITCH clearly labelled, just to avoid any confusion.

There it was – just above and to the right of where he now sat.

"Ok, PAL, I'm going to press the re-start switch!" he declared, in case PAL needed to know. "Three ... oh, what comes after three again?" he said, with slight annoyance at himself.

"Two?" suggested PAL.

"Oh, thanks PAL! … two … one!"

He pressed the green re-start button, which beeped just once in response, whereupon the entire array of computer lights went out and Fatface sat in total darkness inside the windowless Computer Bay.

"Hello?" he said, warily, into the stony silence.

He began to breathe hard as he fumbled around with his gloved puss-paws.

"Oh, help! I'm in a Black Hole!" he yelped, in a sudden panic.

Just then, a whirring sound filled the Computer Bay, and within moments a whole flight deck of lights came flashing back to life with all sorts of clicks and buzzes.

"Restart complete," said PAL, expressionlessly.

That's a relief! thought Fatface. *Now all I've got to do is press the Poop Bay Door button.*

Amongst all the knobs and switches sat a big blue one that said 'PBD' which, (Fatface had been instructed), stood for 'Poop Bay Door'.

"Ok, PAL. I'm going to press this button, and hopefully the Poop Bay Door will now open."

"Affirmative," replied PAL, frostily.

"Ok!" said Fatface. "Here goes! One ... two ... er ... three!"

He pressed the PBD button, and a side panel slid down, revealing a small Picture Box screen.

"Oh great!" he blurted. "Can we watch a movie, PAL? I love *Born Free* ... if you've got it, that is ..."

Ignoring Fatface's request, the screen flickered on, revealing the outside of I-STINC's Poop Bay Door, which could clearly be seen to be opening.

"It worked!" declared a jubilant Fatface.

"Jettisoning ... contents," announced PAL, pausing as if to avoid saying: *'pooperlooper bags'*.

Mesmerised by the image on the screen, Fatface stared in awe at the majestic sight of a parade of innumerable pooperlooper bags that had begun to stream out from I-STINC's Poop Bay in a continuous, swirling ribbon of multi-colours.

"Would you like to know what's going to happen to the ... cargo?" said PAL, in a strange, quiet and slightly unnerving tone, which only made Fatface feel that perhaps he *didn't* want to know.

However, he felt he *ought* to know.

"Er ... yes? I think ..." he said, feeling slightly confused.

"Destination of cargo: The Sun. Arrival Date: approximately three years, where complete disintegration will occur."

Fatface watched as the endless stream of bags twirled and twisted out from the Poop-Bay.

"Well, at least that now explains *dark matter*," he observed, thoughtfully.

With the very last pooperlooper bag leaving I-STINC's shadowy tomb, Fatface watched the small screen as the Poop Bay Door once again closed, at least for the foreseeable future until the next shipment would be launched from CATBASE.

His thoughts turned once again to his present situation – more specifically to the red flashing light on his Wristcom.

'OXYGEN LEVEL: CRITICAL!!'

His opinion of this 'oxygen' stuff had diminished considerably, and seeing how far CATSULE 1 had drifted away from I-STINC only made the news less welcome to his, or more accurately, Furballs' eyes and ears.

"Do you have a return permit?"

A distinctly sinister edge had crept into PAL's voice.

"Come again?" said Fatface, feeling somewhat unnerved. "Er … I didn't know I *needed* a return permit!" he defended, as he timidly began to edge his way around the Bay wall toward the small, closed hatch.

"Do you like cat food?" said PAL, adding, "Yum!" for additional effect, which Fatface felt was unnecessary as he was already beginning to feel **very** uncomfortable.

"You know, I could turn the oxygen off just like that!" said the computer, flippantly.

There followed an unexpected, maniacal laugh.

"I'd ... er ... rather you didn't!" replied Fatface, shakily, as he carefully put his Head Potty back on, trying not to make any sudden movements.

"You know others have been here, and they never go home!" added PAL, in a way that suggested the computer wanted his captive to enquire further.

Oh, chirping chipmonks! thought Fatface. *I need to get out of here!*

"All it takes is just a *flip* of a switch!" continued PAL, nonchalantly and seemingly lost in some sort of computer delirium. "Well," it added, hastily, "I see you are leaving, Commander Fatface! And you know what *THAT* means, don't you?"

Fatface really didn't want to know, but felt it perhaps wise to humour PAL.

"Well, er ... what *does* it mean?" he enquired, wishing he hadn't.

"MUTINY!!" came PAL's acerbic reply.

Oh, help!

FATFACE & FURBALLS' VERY BAD FURDAY

Before Fatface could think of some reassuring (yet untrue) words about wanting to remain with PAL, he clicked his Head Potty back into place, glanced down at his Wristcom, and grimaced.

'OXYGEN LEVEL: NOT MUCH LEFT NOW!'

Breathing as shallowly as he could, he began to hear a strange noise, like someone humming a tune. Switching his spacesuit to Internal Audio, the sound of PAL singing a nursery rhyme interspersed with strange laughter, filtered through his earpiece, stopping him cold.

"Twinkle twinkle little star ... ha ha! ... How I wonder what you are ... ha ha ha! ..."

PAL's gone bonkers! thought Fatface, as all the lights and switches in the Computer Bay began to flash in a nonsensical dance of multitudinous colour.

He glanced up at the Picture Box, which had been switched off and was completely blank.

He'd only ever seen one other incident like this at The Shelter, which had involved Burt who, following a minor operation, was still under the influence of the anaesthetic and had spent the whole night 'singing', (I use the term loosely – if you've ever heard a pug sing, then you'll understand), his favourite choice of song being, 'Old Macdonald Had a Farm' but replacing the 'm' at the end of 'farm' with a 't' and laughing drunkenly all night, much to *Cage Number 6's* annoyance, (and sleep deprivation).

As much as Fatface liked Burt, he didn't really want Burt to be the last image in his mind, should his oxygen decide to stop.

So, as PAL continued to 'sing', Fatface crept gingerly over to the main Computer Panel and began to unplug whatever looked like something that could be unplugged.

At first, he noticed no difference, but soon became aware of a slowing down of PAL's increasingly slurred mutterings.

"... TWINK ... LLL ...ha ha! T ... WINK ... LLLE ... he hee! ... ITTTLLL ... ha ha ha ha!! ... STARRRR rarr rarr rarrrrrrrr ..."

Frantically, Fatface pulled at every available plug – except of course the one which said, 'Emergency Door Release: Warning – EXPLOSIVE!'

"... HOW ... I ... WON ... DERRRRRR ..."

It appeared that in order to shut down PAL, mechanical operations would become non-functioning – well, all except the Emergency Door Release, or EDR. However, it was the word 'explosive' that particularly bothered Fatface.

But, well, if it does explode, I guess I won't know much about it! he thought, stoically, as he tried to maintain focus whilst pulling out everything and anything that seemed pull-outable.

His Wristcom flashed up at him:

'OXYGEN LEVEL: WHAT OXYGEN?' it said, gleefully, although Fatface wasn't sure whether it was being serious or simply trying to make him feel better with a 'joke'. Either way, he got the message.

Having pulled out every wire, plug and switch within reach, he sidled over to the Emergency Door, strapped himself in and placed his gloved paw delicately over the big red EDR button.

Just as PAL got to the final … "WHAT … YOOOOOU …", and was about to sing the last word, "… ARE," Fatface squeezed his eyes tightly shut, held his breath, and pressed.

He wasn't sure quite what happened next, but when he opened his eyes again the Emergency Door was no longer there, and having been exposed to the vacuum of Space, PAL appeared to have stopped singing too. In fact, PAL appeared to have stopped doing anything, as all lights had gone out and all that remained was a lifeless bank of dead switches.

Without delay, Fatface climbed out of the Computer Bay and, turning himself around, clung to the outside of the gargantuan stony-cold cube, resigned to his fate, having decided to at least spend his final moments watching the world go by four hundred kilometres beneath him, thinking of his short life and those things that had mattered the most to him.

Yet, there really was only *one* memory that had meant anything at all. And that was the day he'd met his friend, Furballs – that little, nameless stray kitty, boldly marching down the street with a dead mouse in his mouth.

CHAPTER 15 – A TAIL-LENGTH FROM HOME

As Fatface stared serenely down, taking in the magnificent view of the planet below, a strange streak of light appeared, hurtling upwards from the surface. The Moon was just beginning to rise over Earth's distant sweeping horizon, and the even-more-distant Sun shone its steady, eternal daylight.

Although he was starting to feel rather sleepy, somehow Fatface couldn't take his gaze from that thin trail of light that seemed to be climbing higher and higher.

I hope they're not sending up another Catstronaut! he thought, suddenly feeling a bit worried about the fact that PAL was, well ... no more, and that the Computer Bay's Emergency Door was probably now somewhere on its way to the Moon.

However, the little stream of light pierced Earth's thin blue veil and continued its upward arc into the blackness of Space, where it suddenly veered around in a long, sweeping curve, heading straight toward Fatface.

A slight panic gripped him, causing him to blink several times. Opening his eyes wide, he noticed that the little stream of light was being led by a distinct, conical rocket-shaped solid object which, upon reaching its maximum altitude, suddenly ceased its climb and remained fixed some way beneath him.

That's strange, he thought, as his Wristcom abruptly lit up with a new message:

'SWITCHING TO EMERGENCY AIR SUPPLY. YOU HAVE TEN MINUTES. SORRY I DIDN'T TELL YOU SOONER. I ONLY JUST REMEMBERED I HAD SOME SPARE AIR!'

Oh well. At least I got a little longer than I'd thought, Fatface said to himself. *And, finally, something with some proper air in it too!*

Feeling a little fresher, he stared down at the hovering craft and noticed that something – or some*one*

– seemed to be pressed up against the capsule's little window and was staring back up at him.

Straining to get a closer look, Fatface realised he'd have to let go of I-STINC, and as much as he longed to do so, it didn't seem to be the best option at that particular moment. Nonetheless, he stretched himself as far forward as his tether would allow, at which instant an odd noise began to trickle into his Snoopy Poopy Cap.

"Flo ... (crackle, crackle) ... ting ... (crackle, hiss) ... flea ... (hiss, crackle) ... bags ... (pop, hiss) ... at ... ace! ... (buzz, pop) ... it's ... (crackle, buzz) ... me! ... (pop, hiss) ... urr ... alls!"

The scratchy voice appeared to have a familiar tone, although Fatface couldn't actually understand any of what was being said. He glanced down at his Wristcom. A light was flashing:

'INCOMING MESSAGE. SHALL I ACCEPT?'

He pressed the 'AFFIRMATIVE' button, and a babbling voice erupted into his Head Potty.

"Doglog entry, stardate ... arrgh! Munching meatballs! Who cares about the stardate?! Hey, buddy, it's me!"

"Furballs?" queried Fatface.

He knew there was only one being on Earth (or above it) who would say such a thing as *munching meatballs*. The question was, *what* was he doing up here in Space?

"Yeah! Waddaya know!" replied Furballs, with a slightly nervous laugh.

"Can't live without me, eh?" said Fatface, with an equally shy guffaw.

"Well, you know I couldn't trust you to complete this mission up here all by yourself!" bellowed Furballs, his old acerbic wit now tempered with a light sprinkling of modesty. "I won this horrible contest," he continued, "with pins and pipe cleaners where pins and pipe cleaners *ain't* supposed to go. Anyhows, the prize was this trip to Outer Space!"

He hesitated whilst trying to think of words that would not sound *too* alarming.

"And back?" offered Fatface, filling in the silence.

"Yeah, about that. Did they tell yooz …?"

Furballs didn't get to finish his sentence.

"Not especially," replied Fatface, stoically. "But I kind of gathered this would be a one-way ticket for me."

He coughed, uneasily.

"I know I'm not that important," he continued, softly, with a shrug. "But," he added, rapidly changing the subject, "I got to see my best buddy *and* the whole world! What more could anyone want?"

"Hey!" snapped Furballs, sharply. "No more *past tense one-way-ticket* talk! Yooz have **no** idea what I put myself through for this! I'm coming to get ya, and we're goin' home! Only problem is, my spacecraft won't go any higher."

"Yeah," said Fatface, "and I don't even *have* a spacecraft anymore! I managed to disengage the onboard PAL computer. It went nuts on me. Now I'm just drifting, and I'm gonna be floating around here for the foreseeable future. Who says we get nine lives, eh?"

"Ok, buddy," said Furballs, decisively, "let's think this through! All we have to do is meet halfway, and I can reel you back in with me, and we can go home. Nevermind who's got who's body. At least we'll be ... well, together ..."

Uncharacteristically, Furballs went a bit quiet.

"... And ... er ... by the way," he added, his voice becoming more reticent with each word, "I think you're the *bravest* friend I've ever had."

He didn't have to wait long for a reply.

"I'm the *only* friend you've ever had," said Fatface, simply.

"Ok, don't rub it in!" scolded Furballs, already feeling rather deflated. "But, listen, I was wrong about you! And I'm ..."

The word he wanted to say appeared to be stuck somewhere halfway up his insides.

Come on Furballs! It's now or never! he said, berating himself.

A slight feeling of shame made his voice wobble a bit. But, at last, out it came:

"... I'm ... er ... *sorry* for all the bad things I said to you."

He then cleared his throat, and sniffed a couple of uncomfortable sniffs as a great silence filled the space between them.

Well, for a few seconds, anyway.

Something was happening inside Furballs; something he was unaccustomed to but which he was now finding *extremely* uncomfortable. And he couldn't stop it from bubbling up.

Some odd noises filtered through into Fatface's Snoopy Poopy Cap.

"What's that sound? Is that you, Furballs? ..." he said whilst banging the side of his Head Potty a couple of times to make sure it wasn't misbehaving.

"... Are you ... *crying?*"

Instantly, a sonic tidal wave blasted into Fatface's earpiece:

"BLAAAHHHHH-BOO-HOOOOO!! (Sniff, snuffle, sniff sniff)."

This was immediately followed by the sound of a desperate gasp of air being sucked pitifully inward in little jerky gulps. Fatface sensed it hadn't quite finished and, bracing himself, was rewarded with a second (and somewhat more violent) eruption:

"BLAAAHH HHAAAAAAA! AARRRGGHHH! BOOOHHOOOOOO!! OHHHHHHH! WOAAHHHH! BLAHA-HA..... HA... HA! ... (sniff sniff)."

It eventually dried up to a few, final snuffle-like whimpers, which quickly fizzled into a blunt silence.

"No," lied Furballs, somewhat defensively, having eventually recovered after a muted pause due to him still feeling a bit wobbly.

"Oh ... ok," replied Fatface, with a sort of confined shrug. (He was too scared to do a proper, full-stretch one inside his spacesuit in case it set off any more of those wasps).

"I just thought I heard you crying ... or *someone*," he added, as casually as he could in order not to embarrass Furballs who, upon hearing this, was just about to snap back with a sarcastic blast of, *'Oh, like everyone else who's up here?',* when the thought of the effort this would take, measured against the pay-off of being right seemed like an unwise waste of whatever energy he had left.

Besides, he no longer felt a great need to prove his superior feline cleverness, especially as he currently was – technically speaking – still a pooch.

More than anything, though, Furballs didn't really *want* to say unkind things to Fatface anymore, even if he *was* smarter.

"Oh, alright then. I admit it. Yes, it *was* me!" he grumped, at last, feeling more embarrassed than ever.

Several moments passed as the two space cadets hovered above planet Earth, which spun serenely and majestically beneath them some four hundred kilometres below, (or … three hundred and ninety-nine point nine in Furballs' case).

"Well, guess I don't got much more to say about that," he concluded, in his bestest grammar as he let out a deflated, relieved sigh.

Fatface nodded soberly inside his Head Potty.

"Me too," he agreed, adding, "I know you never really meant those things."

"Thanks, Fatface," said Furballs, brightening up a bit and nodding quietly to himself.

A sudden realisation flashed into his mind.

"Jumping jellyfish, Fatface!" he announced, with a flourish. "You've saved the whole *planet* from disaster! You're all *over* the Picture Box, and you've got five billion followers on *Instacat!*"

"So, it worked then?" said Fatface, humbly.

"Yeah, boy it worked!" replied Furballs, unapologetically. "They're already preparing to launch the next shipment of pooperlooper bags!"

"Oh?" said Fatface, with a bit of a gulp. "In that case, someone had better let them know that the Computer Bay door blew away and is now on its way to the Moon, and ... well ... basically ..."

He went a bit quiet.

"... ahem ... they'll need to install a new PAL computer ..."

Almost whispering, he cleared his throat and added, "... preferably one that doesn't know any songs."

"Songs?" queried Furballs, somewhat nervously. "Don't talk to me about songs! I don't think I *ever* want to hear another song again! And PLEASE don't ask me to sing!"

"Well, I wasn't actually going to right now," replied Fatface, bluntly. "And besides, it would only be a waste of air, or that oxygen stuff ..."

Furballs let out a relieved groan.

"OK, good! No songs! Just give me a moment ole' buddy whilst I put my spacesuit on," he said, chirpily. "Man, I tell ya, it's such a relief to be outta that weirdy cat costume!"

"What weirdy cat costume?" said Fatface, somewhat puzzled.

"Never mind!" answered Furballs. "I'll tell yooz later!"

In a flash, Furballs reappeared outside the Tailstar Rocketplane in his slightly modified spacesuit, (which had been originally designed with the feline form in mind), secured his tether, and prepared to push himself off *freestyle* to meet Fatface halfway.

Fatface, likewise, had made the same preparations his end of things.

"Ok, buddy," radioed Furballs, "I'll count to three, and then let's *DOOZ* this! One … two …"

He stopped.

"Oh! Wait! I forgot something!"

It was the little flower that Lotty had given him. Darting back into Tailstar's small capsule, he instantly reappeared, looking no different.

"What did you do?" queried Fatface.

"You'll see!" replied Furballs, excitedly.

"Just one last thing!" said Fatface, hurriedly.

"What's that?"

"Just don't tail-puff in your suit," he warned, earnestly. "It'll set off all sorts of horrible wasps and blaring lights."

"Yeah, okay … er … thanks for that," said Furballs, uncertainly. "I'll bear that in mind. Now, are yooz ready or are yooz ready?" he queried, somewhat insistently.

"Er ... I think so," said Fatface, feeling not quite as ready as he would have liked but eager nonetheless to leave the metal monolith behind.

"One ... two ... three!"

With hind legs bent, each pushed himself off frog-style, like two uncoiled springs launching themselves from their respective vessels, spreading their front space-suited paws out like wild birds in full-winged flight, gliding serenely toward the other in a silent space ballet.

"Ok," said Fatface, "start using your PJP."

"What's that?" said Furballs.

"There's a small button on the end of each of your front legs."

"Oh, yeah, got it!"

"Don't use too much in one go!" warned Fatface.

Furballs pushed – first his left PJP, which sent him careening off to one side – then his right PJP, which sent him flying back to where he'd started.

"Oh, great," he said, grimly, "that's twenty percent used up already!"

"Little squirts! Little squirts!" urged Fatface, with great authority. "And save that oxygen stuff! Apparently it's important!"

"I'm trying! I'm trying!" yelped Furballs, as he zig-zagged about, squirting first his left PJP and then his right whilst all four limbs swung this way and that. "None of my legs seems to want to talk to the others!"

"Just keep it coming, good buddy!" encouraged Fatface. "Just keep it coming! Just a little squirt from each front leg! And try to use the same amount of propellant for each squirt! Steady as you go!"

"I can't concentrate if yooz keep talking!" countered Furballs, as he wavered about, gradually gaining more control.

"I'm just trying to help!" offered Fatface.

"I know, I know," conceded Furballs, "but these pooch feet just ain't as easy to aim as my feline paws!"

"Just stretch out as far as you can!" urged Fatface.

"I'm tryin', I'm tryin'!" countered Furballs, as he wobbled about, attempting to steady himself.

"You just need to keep your front legs straight!" added Fatface, aware that both animals' PJP supply would soon run out. "Just stretch them out as if you're about to pounce on a ball of string!"

Without questioning further, Furballs lunged forward.

"That's good!" said Fatface. "Now just keep it steady!"

"Will yooz stop talking and let me concenterate!" screeched Furballs, hoping that would be the last word on the matter.

"Just keep your paws outstretched!" said Fatface, optimistically.

"I GOT it! I GOT it!" squawked Furballs, at full stretch. "You try doing this in an oversized pooch-suit!"

"Well, I must admit," said Fatface, "this skinny catsuit is pretty versatile! I just need to be careful not to puncture my suit with those spindly needles you call claws!"

And as they approached each other, the two white spacesuits stretched forth their front paws in an attempt to grasp the other's glove.

FATFACE & FURBALLS' VERY BAD FURDAY

"I got ya! I got ya!" exclaimed Fatface, as he swiped some empty space.

"Noze you don't!" squealed Furballs.

With a couple of frantic sweeps, each snatched a good-sized slice of empty vacuum, missing paws by a fraction of a fur strand's width. And with an abrupt jolt, their tethers reached their furthest stretch, which sent the two Catstronauts yo-yoing back toward their respective spacecraft.

"NO!!" they howled, in unison.

"What do I dooz?" yelled Furballs.

"Just relax!" shouted Fatface.

"Relax?!!" wailed Furballs.

"Yeah, my self-help book said something about staying calm in Adver City, wherever *that* is," replied Fatface, helpfully.

"Yeah, and did it also say anything about what to do when you're suspended three hundred and ninety-nine point nine kilometres above a planet with no air left?" countered Furballs, somewhat anxiously, having a good idea of what the answer might be.

Making a soft landing upon the metal hull, Fatface instantly pushed himself once again off I-STINC and headed back towards Furballs, who had likewise bounced himself off Tailstar, both heading directly toward each other with slightly more elegance than before.

"Use your PJPs!" ordered Fatface, as he wavered this way and that.

"Gotcha!" replied Furballs, who likewise zigged and zagged headfirst toward Fatface.

"When the tether pulls tight, just fire your PJP so you don't bounce backwards again!" instructed Fatface.

"I knowz! I knowz!" said Furballs, agitatedly. "I'm trying to concenterate!"

Each fired little awkward squirts of flame until, eventually, they both became motionless.

"We did it!" announced Fatface, humbly.

"Mmm … not *quite,*" concluded Furballs.

Both looked down at two flashing red lights on their Wristcoms.

"PAW JET PROPELLANT EXPUNGED. IN OTHER WORDS, YOU AIN'T GOT NONE LEFT!"

As a grim realisation began to dawn, each slowly lifted his Head Potty to face the other.

The two animals remained in silent suspension, Head Potty to Head Potty, so close were they that each could see through the other's visor to the alter-ego within.

Given that, away from Earth's gravity in the vacuum of Space, there is nothing for a motionless object to push against to make it move, and having used up every drop of PJP in each one's quest to reach the other, the fact remained that if either one disconnected his tether, he would simply remain where he was.

The small (yet significant) space between them may as well have been a million light years. For, with no PJP left and their tethers having halted their forward motion, both space farers floated tantalisingly close to each other in the frictionless vacuum of space, and yet excruciatingly out of reach.

"One lousy tail-length!" spewed Furballs. "The one time a feline needs a ball of string! One of us should've kept some PJP!"

"That *is* a good idea," enthused Fatface before stopping abruptly. "Well, it *would've* been," he muttered, with a dismal *humph* a few moments later, having thought it through a bit more.

Furballs checked his Wristcom.

'FIVE MINUTES OF AIR LEFT ... AND COUNTING! HAVE A NICE DAY!"

"Ok, listen to me, Furballs," asserted Fatface, unexpectedly. "The only way I see it is like this: I divert whatever air I've got left to my PJPs, cut my tether, fire a few squirts, and then you catch me! Simples!"

"That's a stupid plan!" snapped Furballs, staring hard into Fatface's visor. "How are you gonna breathe if you've got no air left?"

Fatface scratched his Head Potty.

"Listen, if my calculations are correct, I can hold my breath for ... well ... I forgot exactly how long. But, remember, I made a new World Record in my training at Catbase!"

Furballs huffed, partly out of envy that Fatface had achieved such a high accolade, but mostly from thinly disguised pride that Fatface had been wearing *his* catsuit at the time.

"So," concluded Fatface, "all you've got to do is catch me and reel me in with you! How hard can *that* be?"

It was the *'all you've got to do'* part that Furballs wasn't too keen on, as if reeling your best buddy along a one hundred metre stretch of thin rope whilst wearing a slippery spacesuit far above your planet while your buddy holds his breath was just an everyday thing that happens all the time.

What could possibly go wrong? thought Furballs, as he tried to ignore the horrible churning in his stomach. *Just about everything!* he replied to himself, glumly.

Fatface looked down at his Wristcom which, with great jollity, displayed the message:

'OUT OF AIR IN ... THREE MINUTES! ENJOY IT WHILE YOU CAN!'

"So," he said, mimicking Furballs' words, "shall we dooz this?"

Furballs went to reply, but for some reason he just didn't feel like saying anything. Instead, both animals simply sighed as they floated silently above the blue planet.

"Look," said Fatface, at last, "we both know at least *one* of us has a very *good* chance of being on a one-way ticket here, or a very *bad* chance of getting home, never mind getting his own body back."

Furballs stared silently and bleakly out through his visor.

"If I don't make it," continued Fatface, solemnly, "then I won't be able to give you your body back, and I'm really sorry about that. And, if I *do* happen to get through the next few minutes but am then unable to give you your body back due to the fact that we haven't managed to find the Time-Travelling Dudey Guy, then I guess me and you will always be a little bit of me and a little bit of … well … you, and I'll have to call you Furface from now on."

Furballs thought for a moment.

"And I'll have to call you Fatballs," he said, flatly.

In unison, the two animals let out joint sighs and stared out at the vastness surrounding them.

"Hey," continued Furballs, brightening up slightly, "do you think there's anyone else out there? Or are we it?"

They both gazed around at the expanse of Space and stars.

"I dunno," replied Fatface, "it's very pretty from here. I don't see why we'd need to go anywhere else, really."

"I wonder how they spell 'pooperlooper' in Africa," pondered Furballs, peering down at the vast continent as it sailed serenely by in full splendour.

"I guess there's a *lot* of that down there with all those elephants and dinosaurs stomping about," replied Fatface, earnestly.

"There aren't any dinosaurs!" said Furballs, bluntly, without offering further explanation. "Besides," he added, "you've been watching Born Free *waaaaay* too much!"

He paused. "You're right though," he resumed, "we're just a little dot in this big empty space, aren't we? A little dot of pooperlooper."

"Yeah," said Fatface, "but if we weren't here at all, there'd be no one to enjoy the view! And the bigger the view, the better it looks. That's why we're small ... you know ... so we can appreciate how *big* everything is! And in a weird way, it's almost as if you and me were *supposed* to be up here."

The two animals checked their Wristcoms, and sighed.

'OUT OF AIR IN ... TWO MINUTES!' said the readout. 'I'D GET BACK TO THE SHIP IF I WERE YOU!'

"Yeah, you're right, Fatface," said Furballs, ignoring the Wristcom's dim forecast. "But, do you know what I really want?"

"What's that?"

"I mean, what I really, *truly*, with all my heart, want?"

He didn't wait for a reply.

313

"… A home. A *real* home."

"Yeah, just imagine," gushed Fatface, "me being taken for walks, and you being put out every night – *all* night – and getting into fights with the other cats! A *real* home. Soft, *clean* bed to sleep on, cosy nights in by the fire …"

"And a real catflap of my own," sighed Furballs, longingly.

"Maybe it's better to stay up here after all," mused Fatface. "I've dreamed of these things since I can remember. And all I've had is … well … all *we've* had is …"

"Oh gosh! I wish I was back in The Shelter now!" blubbed Furballs.

"Really? Don't you want your own catflap?" queried Fatface. "Like, who's gonna buy *me* a dogflap? Dogs are trapped – at their owner's beck and call. Put on a leash – yuck!"

"Yeah, and loved, and cuddled, and spoken to," said Furballs. "I even heard some pooches get to *sleep* with their owners!"

"Eeewww, that's gross!" agreed Fatface. "Hoomans are *weeeiiird!*"

"Waddaya say, ole' buddy?" said Furballs, with a sudden spring in his voice. "Wanna go home? I don't wanna stay here and watch you ....er..."

"Er, yeah, me neither," replied Fatface, in full agreement.

"Well," said Furballs, decisively, "I guess being alive in *your* body is better than not being alive at all! And we're not gonna find that Time-Travelling Dudey Guy anytime soon here! Anyway, first things first."

"Huh?"

"I gotta take a leak. Did you get the Standard Issue Cat Nappy?"

"Oh, man!" groaned Fatface.

(A few seconds later ...)

"All done!" said Furballs. "Ready as I'll ever be! You know, whatever happens in the next few seconds, I'm proud to have yooz as my friend."

"Thanks, Furballs," agreed Fatface, humbly, adding, "you know what I'm going to say, don't you ...?"

"Yeah, I know," said Furballs, reluctantly, "you're gonna say that you're my *only* friend."

Feeling a little embarrassed, he cleared his throat with a slight cough and concluded, "Well, let's save the BFF talk for later. You ready?"

"Ready!" came Fatface's reply.

"Well, ok then, let's dooz this!" said Furballs, with his more usual gusto.

"OK," said Fatface. A sudden pensiveness filtered out through his voice. "So, I'm cutting the tether now! Here goes!"

Taking one deep breath, he diverted his remaining air to his PJPs. Careful not to tear his spacesuit, he then grabbed the space-knife that was attached to his space-belt, cut his tether, and gave two, precise squirts.

"I-STINC no more!" he declared, silently to himself as he launched himself at Furballs, who instinctively splayed out his gloved front paws as wide as he could in order to catch Fatface.

I'm coming home! thought Fatface, as he gleefully lurched first one way then the other whilst Furballs swiped frantically, (and almost always slightly too late).

"Keep it steady!" howled Furballs, as he desperately tried to guess which way Fatface would turn.

I'm comin' home! Fatface repeated silently to himself, as he held his breath with puffed-out cheeks. *Or maybe I'm not!* he added, just as the last squirt of his PJP sent him veering off at a slightly sharper incline than he'd intended.

"I thought you said you'd calculacerated your angles!" shouted Furballs, with an agonising groan. "You need to go further to the right! Bouncing beeburps, Fatface, what are yooz *doing*?!"

But it was too late.

Fatface had most definitely miscalculated his angles, and now appeared to be heading toward the constellation of Orion.

Furballs' heart began to thump hard in his chest, and he began to blink disbelievingly at the growing gap between him and his fellow space explorer, watching helplessly as Fatface drifted silently away, his radio signal fading into broken blips of noise.

Then, nothing.

And he began to sob.

"FATFACE!!!" he wailed, disconsolately to a muted silence as the little white figurine with his Head Potty got smaller and smaller until he became just a little white dot, no bigger than the pinpoints of light into which he merged.

"NO!! OH! FATFACE!! WHAT AM I GONNA DOOOOOZ WITHOUT YOU? I CAN'T LIVE WITHOUT YOU! OH! FATFACE!"

Eventually the tears stopped, and an exhausted Furballs reluctantly began to haul himself back down his tether to his spacecraft.

I don't know why I'm even bothering! he moped, as he re-entered Tailstar, flipped the Artificial Gravity Switch to 'ON', and flopped down in the luxury window seat just as an array of tasty feline snacks and morsels, (which on any other day would have been most welcome), automatically unfurled from a side compartment and sat, unacknowledged.

Oh, this is unbearable! thought Furballs, completely disregarding the banquet before him.

Feeling bereft as he was with his mumblings and misery, he had failed to notice what looked like dwarf planet Pluto hovering nearby to the I-STINC space station above him.

A faint crackle broke the silence in his headset.

Probably NASSA wanting to know my whereabouts!

Yet, as he listened, there was something about the crackly voice that seemed *very* familiar.

"Tailstar 1, come in please!" it said.

I knowz that voice! thought Furballs, quizzically.

"Tailstar 1, come in!"

He staggered over to the Communications Console.

"Yeah?" he said, flatly.

"Oh, Mr. Furballs, I presume?"

"Not so much of the *Mister*," he said, disinterestedly. "Furballs ain't my second name!"

Come to that, it ain't my first name, either, he thought, gloomily.

"Oh, well, yes of course, Furballs it is!"

"Who is this? And how do yooz know my name, anyhows?" he said, huffily.

I ain't got time for this ....

"Well, you might remember me from The Shelter. I'm the Time Traveller who needed the loo?"

Furballs raced to the little window and glared angrily up at the hovering dwarf planet.

"You!" he scowled. "YOU!" he scowled, again. "YOOOOZ!" he erupted, still scowling. "If it wasn't for YOU, I'd still have my BUDDY!"

"Oh, about that ..." started the Time Traveller.

He didn't get very far.

"DON'T you give me 'ABOUT THAT'!" snapped Furballs, searching desperately around the Navigation Console for anything he could throw. "It's because of YOU and your stoopid *PLASMA-BALLEE-THINGY* that I've lost the only friend I ever had!"

He made a big huffing noise, then plonked himself down in the pilot's seat.

"Well, I guess you won't want to speak to him then," said the Time Traveller, nonchalantly.

"I'd *love* to speak to him," said Furballs, with a searing ache in his voice, "but he's halfway to the Great Dog in the Sky by now! And I'll never ..."

"DO stop all this snivelling!" interrupted the Time Traveller. "I can't bear it! And besides, there's absolutely no need for it!"

"Yeah, well yooz never had a friend like I did!" challenged Furballs, as he picked up the little flower that Lotty had given him.

I was going to give this to him!

"This is true," continued the Time Traveller, slightly sniffly, "which is why I spend my time – oops, no pun intended! – travelling the Galaxy helping people and animals like you!"

"Well, thanks for ..."

Furballs went to say 'nothing', but the word got stuck halfway up (again).

"... Did yooz just say something about me not wanting to speak to Fatface?"

"Well!" said the Time Traveller. "I've been standing here for the past five minutes *trying* to tell you ..."

"Tell me *what?*" said Furballs, stretching up to look through his little triangular window.

"Well, I've been *trying* to tell you that ... well ... he's ..."

But before the Time Traveller could finish his sentence, a familiar voice penetrated the crackly atmosphere of the radio waves as Furballs craned his neck as far as he could, only to see 'Pluto' hovering opposite Tailstar's main window.

"Hey, buddy! It's me!"

Furballs staggered back to his chair, and gripped the sides.

"Fatface?"

"Hold on! I'm coming to the door!"

There, in Pluto's open doorway, exposed to the cold, airless vacuum of space, stood the ghostly figure of what appeared to be Furball's catsuit, currently being occupied by what sounded like Fatface, (minus his spacesuit, which he'd somehow lost).

"How are you *doing* this?" said Furballs, feeling rather faint at the sight of Pluto's open doorway, but even *more* faint at the sight of the one standing *in* it.

"Oh, it's just an old Time Traveller's trick, you know!" said the Time Traveller. "Force-fields and all that ancient stuff! Easy when you know how!"

"Well," replied Furballs, "it's a neat trick, but ... is that really *you* Fatface?" he said, somewhat hesitantly to the ghostly mirage hovering in the opposite space door.

"Yeah, waddaya know!" said Fatface, nonchalantly. "I was just drifting off across Space, thinking that was it, and just thinking about you and me and The Shelter and our adventures, when the Time-Travelling Dudey Guy swoops across in his Time Machine Pluto Thingy and grabs me! Next thing I know, I've lost my spacesuit but somehow I'm breathin' again and standing here talking to you!"

"I'm feeling a bit … well … wobbly," said Furballs, as he melted down gingerly into his chair, still gripping the sides. "Do you have *any* idea how I felt back there? Just seeing yooz float off … you know … *forever.*"

Before Fatface had a chance to reply, the Time Traveller stepped forward.

"Well, Furballs," he said, eagerly, "are you coming across?"

"Er, thanks, but I think I've had enough *Space Travel* for one lifetime!"

"No!" said the Time Traveller. "I don't mean via a piece of *string!* I mean via Transmigrational Electrostatic Quantum Energisation?" He paused for an affirmative response. "You know," he said, finally to the silence, "Teleportation!"

"Oh, *that*," said Furballs, flatly, and none the wiser. "And don't talk to me about string!" he grumped.

"So," concluded the man, "I can then return you both to your rightful bodies, and, well, take you home!"

Home? I don't got no home! thought Furballs.

He weighed up his options.

324

Either that Time-Travelling Dudey Guy is playing tricks on me, and that's not really Fatface and I'll end up in some weirdy freak place where Time-Travelling Dudey Guys hang out.

A small nudge of optimism prodded his insides.

*Or ... maybe he's for real, and that really **is** my ole' buddy. Oh, boy! I saw him float away! How can that really be him? Well, I guess I don't got much to lose ...*

"Let's dooz this thing!" he said, finally, and before he'd even finished his sentence he found himself standing inside Pluto's doorway, which had a sign above it saying:

'MALFUNCTION!'

"Yeah ... er ... what's *that* for?" queried Furballs, blinking under the bright lights of Pluto's interior.

"Oh, that's nothing!" replied the Time Traveller. "I've been meaning to get that sign fixed for ages – literally!"

Once again, he made his familiar *laugh-snort-laugh-snort-snort* sound.

Adjusting to the light, Furballs lowered his paw from his eyes and looked quizzically across at the one who stood before him.

"Is that really *you*, Fatface?" he said.

"Yeah, I guess," replied Fatface.

"Yeah, that's definitely you!" said Furballs. "If yooz ain't sure who yooz are, then that is most definitely yooz!"

"Well, shall we get to work then?" said the Time Traveller, as he clapped his hands together brusquely.

"Yeah, let's *dooz* this!" the two space cadets bellowed, as they high pawed each other.

"Now, the first thing I need to say to you," began the man, "is to say that it was absolutely crucial that I land here at precisely the instant I did. I realise I had something to do with the whole High Residual Plasma Ball anomaly, but ..."

He coughed, slightly awkwardly.

"... I *did* warn you both *not* to touch it!"

"Yeah, well, it's a BIT LATE now!" offered Furballs.

"Yes, yes! I realise that! So can we just get on with the procedure?"

"Procedure?" said Fatface, slightly nervously.

"It's perfectly safe, and it shouldn't hurt!" exclaimed the Time Traveller.

"Shouldn't hurt?" said Furballs, with a bit of a wobble, the memory of all those *pins* still wincingly fresh in his mind.

"Well, not much ..." added the man, albeit slightly under his breath. "By the way," he continued, "you won't see me again. I've been promoted, and am on my way to the ceremony now! I would invite you both, but it's *way* too far into the future. They've made me ..."

He wiped a grateful tear.

"... a Time Lord! And ... I get an 'on-board' loo! The Time Lords Council of The Local Group of Galaxies, Sector 2, said they were *so* impressed with what I had done with Pluto, but that they were fed up with me mucking up Spacetime with my unauthorised toilet stops! So, they have installed a state-of-the-art Timeportaloo just for me! It's made all the difference!

And that means … ahem … no more Residual Plasma Balls! Well, are you both ready?"

"Ready ain't our problem!" said Furballs, bluntly, as he and Fatface closed their eyes for the last time in each other's bodies.

CHAPTER 16 — HOME SWEET SHELTER

"Ahhh! It feels so good to be back in my own fur! Thanks for looking after me!"

Fatface stretched a full-length stretch, then gave himself a good canine shake from head to tail.

"No problemo!" said Furballs, having just given himself a good wash, (the first of many for the day), and was now relaxing in his basket with a copy of 'Cats & Dogs Can Be Friends Weekly'.

It was just another normal day back at The Shelter, and the familiar sounds, (and smells), filled the two strays with a feeling of comfort and safety.

"I guess we're back home again!" said Fatface, stretching luxuriantly across his grubby old basket.

The solitary Picture Box, high up on the wall outside *Cage Number 6,* rattled on unheeded with its News report of the daring mission by the 'two anonymous catstronauts' who 'single-pawdly' unstuck I-STINC's Poop Bay Door and released the trapped pooperlooper bags, going on to say that if anyone knows of these brave souls' whereabouts, to get in touch, as there is a substantial monetary reward awaiting them.

A familiar voice breezed past the cage.

"Mornin' lads!"

It was Burt.

"Hey, Burt!" said Fatface. "Burt, my boy!" declared Furballs. "Where are you off to?"

"Just going for my 'daily', and to check my weemail," said Burt. "We got a special lady coming today. So, I gots to get meself all puffed and preened up, so the Shelter Lady says. First thing this morning, she's on at me to go and do my toilet! I mean, I'd only just woken up!"

"Oh!" said Fatface. "So, who's this *special lady*, then?"

"Well," said Burt, "you'll find out soon enough!"

And off he went, out to The Yard.

"Furballs, can I ask you a question?" said Fatface, tentatively.

FATFACE & FURBALLS' VERY BAD FURDAY

"Sure!" said Furballs, over his spectacles, (which he'd just had fitted upon his return, as some aftereffect of Time Travel had made him a bit blurry).

"You know when you failed to catch me, and I ... er ... when I ... floated away?"

"Yeah," said Furballs, without looking up from his magazine, partly because he was in the middle of reading a particularly interesting article about new research which involved experiments undertaken by human scientists who would be spending time living with families who have cats and dogs, but mostly because he was hoping Fatface wouldn't ask about the one thing he didn't want to discuss.

"Well ..." said Fatface, oblivious to Furballs' thoughts, "... did you ... ahem ... *cry?*"

"Nah!" said Furballs, with a casual sniff, hoping the matter would be dropped.

"Yes, you did! I heard you!" accused Fatface.

"Well, alright, yes I *did* cry! But I didn't *fail* to catch you! YOU failed to be *caught* by me!"

CASS CLARK

He put his magazine down. "Oh heck! What am I sayin'? We did alright, Fatface. Yooz and meez. We did alright. And, yeah, I did ... er, *cry.*"

He paused, then added, hesitantly:

"A bit ... well, a *lot,* actually."

Changing the subject, he shrugged and said, "Here, I got something for yooz!"

"Ooooh, yippee, a prezzie!" applauded Fatface, clapping his paws together a little too hard. "Ouch! I gotta get used to these again!" he said, with slight embarrassment.

Out from his basket, Furballs pulled the little flower that Lotty had given him.

"I meant to give this to you!" he said, handing him the now rather squished, dried-up daisy. "You really are the bravest, bestest friend I've ever had."

Once again, he didn't have to wait long for the predicted reply.

"I'm the *only* friend you've ever had! But, oh, gosh, thanks, Furballs!" said Fatface, as the limp little daisy wilted in his paw. "It's beautiful! That Lotty must be a really sweet and lovely kitty!"

"Yeah," said Furballs, "but I doubt I'll ever see her again," he sighed.

"Well, you got me!" said Fatface, optimistically.

Furballs nodded, defeatedly.

"Yeah, Fatface. I got you!"

*

Later that day, a lovely young girl came to The Shelter with her mum, and instantly fell in love with the occupants of *Cage Number 6*.

"I'll take them both!" said the girl, excitedly to the Shelter Lady. "They can sleep in my room with me and my telescope and my poster of Laika the Space Dog!"

Fatface's heart leapt in his chest.

"My Laika! She's alive!" he yelped, as the girl chuckled with gleeful delight at Fatface's jubilant little dance.

"And I'll take Burt and Pertwee too!" she added. "And they can *all* play with my other cat, my beautiful Persian Blue named Lotty!"

Furballs' eyes lit up.

"Well, things is definitely looking on the up!" he said, not giving a cat's whisker any longer about his grammar.

"And, oh!" announced the girl upon remembering something extremely important whilst pointing through the bars of *Cage Number 6*. "I'll give these two some proper names!"

And off they all went to their new Forever Home, where they lived (mostly) happily ever after, with warm fires to sleep by, their own brand-new beds, deluxe litter trays, wild nights out, (well, for Furballs anyways), and for the now-former occupants of *Cage Number 6*, proper new names. And yes, Furballs *did* finally get his very own catflap!

THE END.

EPILOGUE

Six years later, a solar Coronal Mass Ejection emerged from the Sun, sending a spray of solar particles and remnants from all the pooperlooper bags that had been sent into it. Luckily, it missed planet Earth and instead headed straight for the Moon, (where the latest human settlement had just landed), and splattered their lovely new white space suits with ... well, I think you can guess!

THE PROPER END (AGAIN).

ANIMAL TRANSLATOR

Compiled mostly by Furballs (with additions by Fatface) and with The Correkt Animal Spellinks and also The Way Hoomans Tri To Spell Thinks (Baddly).

Note: No responsibility can be taken by the author for any disappointment experienced for any of these words not appearing in the story or for any disagreements with your schoolteachers over ~~gramma~~ ...ooops! ... grammar, or ~~spellinks~~ ... ooops! ... spellings. Capiche?

Animal Translation:

Word:

Sarcatsick	A mixture of sarcasm and regurgitated food, usually served up without empathy. Furballs
Clarificate	To make things nice and easy-squeezy to comprehendificate, ie. if you 'get it' then you got it! Furballs
Comprehendificate	See 'clarificate'
Poo	<ul><li>Poo (British English)</li><li>Poop (American English)</li><li>Stool (doctor language – and there's me thinking it's a seat! You know, I sat on my STOOL this morning – gross! Furballs)</li><li>Poo poo (baby language).</li><li>Caca (French)</li><li>Poo (German)</li><li>Achterschip (Dutch)</li><li>Cachu (Welsh)</li></ul>

- Bajs (Swedish)
- Mierda (Spanish)
- Kakec (Slovenian)
- Poo (Scots Gaelic)
- Rahat (Romanian)
- изнурять [iznuryat'] (Russian)
- cocô (Portuguese) (Warning to any Portuguese travellers – if someone offers you a nice hot cup of *coco* anywhere outside of Portugal, it's OK TO DRINK! Furballs)
- Rufa (Polish)
- Baesj (Norwegian)
- Kak (Luxembourgish)
- Lakoti (Lithuanian)
- Cacca (Italian)
- Lem (Irish)
- Tat (Hungarian)
- Mut (Albanian)

African Languages
- Poef (Afrikaans)
- Uthuvi (Zulu)
- Tsvina (Shona)
- Kinyesi (Swahili)
- Uthuvi (Zulu)

Middle-Eastern Languages
- براز الانسان [biraz al'iinsan]

(Arabic)

340

- קקי (Hebrew)
- Poz (Kurdish)
- قورت دادن (Persian)

Asian Languages
- 船尾 [chuánwěi] (Chinese Traditional)
- 駄目 (Japanese)
- Poo (Lao)
- Bok. Kaka (Turkmen)
- کو poo (Urdu)
- Poo (Uzbek)
- Người mướn (Vietnamese)
- bok. Kaka (Turkish)
- คนเซอ (Thai)
- पूप (Nepali)
- Поттер (Mongolian)
- Poo (Georgian)

(Austronesian Languages)
- Poo (Cebuano)
- Poo (Maori)
- Pawarto (Javanese)
- Tahi (Malay)
- Buritan (Indonesian)
- Poo (Hawaiian)
- Tae (Filipino)
- Tanoa (Samoan)

Other
- Stercus (Latin)

Furballs	A horrible combination of fur and the contents of a cat's stomach, usually regurgitated up by said cat accompanied by retching sounds and a look of sheer terror upon the cat's face. (Also happens to be the name of one of the main characters).
Hooman	Human. Odd-shaped beings with weirdly placed fur, or sometimes no fur. Long gangly limbs, horribly ugly paws, (especially the ones they stand on with those disgustingly long, spindly things called 'toes'), and ears placed on the *sides* of their heads! I mean, how are you supposed to hunt for your dinner with those lugholes stuck on the *side*? "Shall I go *this* way? Or shall I go *that* way?" (I'm sorry ... I have to go now as I'm now laughing way too much. Furballs)
Catstronaut	A feline astronaut, 'space cat'. (A very cool dude. Furballs)
Fatface	A stray dog with wide features, descended from the great Egyptian Canine Dynasty which bred their pooches specifically with wide, simple, smiley faces to look like they were permanently happy to serve their masters, the Pharaohs, such as: ~~Tutancatmoon~~. Furballs

	Tutancanine (Corrected by Fatface)
BFF	Best Furry Friend
Oesophagus	The throat area, can be used in either direction in cats, birds and anyone who eats the wrong thing.
Scientificatically (1)	Unarguable fact, based upon rigorous investigation, mostly by the feline species (you know, the most intelligent species on this planet and probably most other planets too). Furballs
Uncharactercateristic	Out of character. Behaviour not usually seen in a feline.
Si-mutt-aneously	When a canine (or other animal) does something at the same time that something else is happening. Fatface
Refurred	Described, suggested, mentioned about, passed along. (Or getting a new coat). Furballs
Scientificatically (2)	Empirical evidence of sumfing you can prove

343

	factually (or fa-cat-ually). Furballs
Empurrical	Human spelling: *Empirical.* A fact. Something yooz can actually see. Furballs (See also 'Scientificatically').
Predicatable	Human spelling: *Predictable.* Meaning: You know what's coming … You've heard it all before … Oh, here we go again … etc. Furballs
Sardonicatly	Human spelling: *Sardonically.* Meaning: thinking oneself to have very clever humour but with extreme sarcatcism and even unkind wishes, i.e. heartless humour (the best kind). Furballs
Muttered	Something unkind mumbled so that whomever you're with can't hear you *fully* but *just* enough to be bothered by what you said. "I've been muttered." would be the appropriate remark. Furballs
Simultanee-mouse-ly	At the same time as something else happening.

	but may involve a mouse or something that squeaks. (See also *simuttaneously*). **Fatface**
Bweird	A cross between 'beard' and 'weird', used mostly with regard to anyone with a beard who is ... well ... weird. Furballs
Kitalian	Any feline born in Kitaly, duh! Furballs
Basicatally	In a very simple way (a bit like Fatface, tee-hee!) Furballs
Uncomfartable	Do I really need to explain? Oh alright ... I made it up and it just made me laugh a lot – (yep, still haven't really grown up). But if you insist – it means trapped wind experienced in an inappropriate setting for its release. As a polite way of telling (read: *warning*) anyone present that you are not completely at ease in the *windy* department, it can be helpful to say in advance, "I'm feeling a little uncomfartable." Those around you

	can then choose to remain or depart. **Furballs**
Purrfect	Exquisite characteristic of the feline species. Utter perfection! (Or *purr*-fection). **Furballs**
Catisfaction	Feelin' paw-licking, back-scratchin' gooooooooood! **Furballs**
Irrefurrant	Humour with a slight undertone of rebellious but furry disrespect. The feline species excels at the above (minus the humour). **Fatface** The canine species excels at the above – (minus the intelligence). **Furballs**
Purrspective	Seeing stuff from different positions, either in space, time, or the angle of your fur (see 'Infurmation' below). **Furballs**
Headucated	Information that someone else has put into your head that you never asked for, is of no use, and really doesn't matter anyway. **Furballs**
Infurmation	(a) Your fur's either flat and silky-smooth. Or …

	(b) It sticks up in the air. 'a' tells you all is well. 'b' tells you yooz gotta problem. Furballs
Philosophicatilly	A feline's ability to ponder all those deep thoughts about life, the Universe and everything – like food, and the latest design in catflaps … you know, those sorts of things. Furballs
The 'smarts'	An unexpected attack of intelligence, rarely found in canines. (Did I mention *rarely?* Just wanna be clear on that!) Furballs
Particular Physics	Stuff to do with Quantum Particulars – you know, the little, teeny weeny things of life that REALLY DO matter and that mostly are COMPLETELY disregarded by EVERYONE else, ie. when you do something *KIND* and NO ONE notices. Fatface
Oponion	Human spelling: *Opinion.* This is one of those 'double meaning' words:

	1. When someone thinks they know something but they really don't, yet they say it anyways, and nobody cares a cat's whisker what you just said except you, and you care very deeply about being right. 2. Can also be a point of view that will make your eyes water. Furballs
Confidense	Human spelling: *Confidence.* Meaning: 'With density', ie. doing something EXTREMELY stupid, like ... . (fill in with your own example). Furballs Or ... trying something you're not sure if you can do but until you try it you won't ever know, like .... (fill in with your own example). Fatface
Sumfing	Human spelling: *Something.* Meaning: a thing. Furballs (Alternative meaning: a mathematical answer, ie. A *sum* of *things*, e.g. 2+2=? Oh, what was it again?) Fatface
Purrfectly	Human spelling: *Perfectly.* Meaning: without fault or error. A word usually associated exclusively with the feline species. Furballs

Purrtiklar	Human spelling: *Particular*. Meaning number 1: something precise and worthy of special attention. Meaning number 2: to tickle someone while they purr, or to purr while someone tickles you. Furballs
Catastrophe	Human spelling is the same. A disaster caused by any feline. Fatface
Owtitude	The degree to which something unpleasant is happening, i.e., how much something hurts. Furballs
Happeez	Happy! Furballs (& Fatface too)
Predicatament	Human spelling: *Predicament*. A feline who finds himself or herself in a bit of a pickle. Furballs
Furline	The pile of a feline's coat, that is – if you rub it one way it's smooth, and if you rub it the other way it's ruff (see below). Furballs
Ruff	Human spelling: *Rough*. When your coat's rubbed the wrong way. Furballs

Scientifical	Too clever for the likes of yooz! Furballs
Noze	An emphatic "No!" (in Furballs speak). Furballs
Interfurr	To meddle in someone else's fur which is none of your business! Furballs
Animaloid	Anything that lives and breathes that ain't hoomanoid or vegetabloid. Furballs
Scampurred	Making purring sounds whilst running from someone who has tricked you. "I've been scampurred!" Furballs
Accumulazzerate	Human spelling: *Accumulate.* To gather a pile of stuff you don't really need (such as Fatface's poster collection). **Furballs** (Or Furballs' magazine collection). **Fatface**
Interpurrupting	Human spelling: *Interrupting.* To purr loudly when someone else is talking, and you think you've got

	something better to say than what they're saying so that they get distracted and lose their train of thought. Then, ta da! You step in and say what *you* want to say! Furballs
Distinctiful	Something that's full-up and stinks. Furballs
Discomfiture	Uncomfortableness of the extreme variety. Furballs
Purrfect	Human spelling: *Perfect.* Translation: The absolute height of *bestness* that only a feline can attain. Furballs
Complicatted	Human spelling: *complicated.* Translation: A difficult task that only a bona fide feline could *possibly* have the intelligence to complete or even understand. Furballs
Purp	A cross between 'poo', (or 'poop'), and 'burp'. Animals exclusively use the term 'tail-puff'. Humans call it a 'bottom burp' among other names. Can be used either as a noun or verb, e.g. "Who just did a purp?" (noun) "Me! It was me who purped!" (verb – past tense). Furballs

Gas list	A bit like a 'guess list' – you know, like when you go to a party and you're one of the important ones there, (well, that's never happened to me), but instead it's only certain gases that are invited, e.g. oxygen (welcome), methane (not welcome). **Fatface**
Furternity	A mixture of 'eternity' and 'fur', it basically means you will always have some fur forever and ever (whether you want some or not). **Furballs**
Flip Flop	A music style that is a cross between hip hop, fur, and rubber sandals. **Furballs**
Apologeticatly	A feline's way of saying sorry (in other words, something they NEVER say). **Furballs** Or … A canine's way of saying sorry (in other words, something they ALWAYS say). **Fatface**

ADD YOUR OWN ANIMAL TRANSLATIONS!

Animal Word: Translation:

BLURB OUT-TAKES:

- "If you wanna different view of life ... walk a mile in someone else's paws..."
- "To boldly walk in someone else's paws..."
- "To boldly go where no stray has gone before."
- "PAL! Open the Poop Bay Doors ... MIAOW!"
- "In space no one can hear you poo!"
- "To boldly go where no stray has pooed before!"
- "In space, no one can hear you miaow!"
- "To boldly poo where no stray has pooed before!"
- "To boldly stray where no poo has strayed before!"
- "Life stinks!" "Nope. That's just *you*." (How did that get in here?)

- "To …. (add your own)

  ....

- "To

  ....

  ....

- "To   ....

  ....

- "To ....

  ....

- "To ....

  ....

- "To ....

  ....

358

AUTHOR BIOGRAPHY

I grew up in Kent, an only-child to my milkman Dad and home-help Mum. I was a bit of a daydreamer who dreamt of far-off travel and amazing adventures. I found I loved stargazing, and much later on came an opportunity to travel to Namibia and be an astronomer out in the Namib Desert!

Before that, I taught myself to play guitar (the one in the photo, which I bought for £20 second hand at the age of 13 having saved up my pocket money!). I had always dreamed of writing a book, and Namibia provided the inspiration for my first novel, DJ & The Valley of The Dunes. I have also always loved cetaceans, and support WDC: https://uk.whales.org/ (Whale & Dolphin Conservation). And when I'm not doing all that, I love to ride my motorcycle!

I hope you enjoy reading my stories! You can contact me here: info@song-stories-and-stars.com

I'd love to hear from you!

Your friend, CC.

Other books by the author:

- **DJ & The Valley of The Dunes**

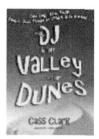

- **Orca Sky – The Girl Who Sang With The Whales**

Website: https://www.song-stories-and-stars.com

Printed in Great Britain
by Amazon

47777089R00212